HOLT Science Spectrum®

Physical Science

Math Skills

HOLT, RINEHART AND WINSTON

A Harcourt Education Company

Orlando • **Austin** • New York • San Diego • London

ISBN-13: 978-0-03-093622-7
ISBN-10: 0-03-093622-5

Print Code   5 6 7 082 10 09 08

Contents

Contents

Skills Worksheet

Math Skills

Conversions

After you study each sample problem and solution, work out the practice problems on a separate sheet of paper. Write your answers in the spaces provided.

PROBLEM

Armando stepped on the scale in his doctor's office and found out that his mass is 35 kg. What is his mass in grams?

SOLUTION

Step 1:   List the given and unknown values.

> **Given:**   *mass in kilograms* = 35 kg
>
> **Unknown:**   *mass in grams* = ? g

Step 2:   Determine the relationship between units. By using the table below, you know that 1 kg = 1,000 g. You will multiply because it takes a lot of grams to make up each kilogram.

Step 3:   Write the equation for the conversion.

$$mass\ in\ g = mass\ in\ kg \times \frac{1,000\ g}{1\ kg}$$

Step 4:   Insert the known values into the equation, and solve.

$$mass\ in\ g = 35\ \cancel{kg} \times \frac{1,000\ g}{1\ \cancel{kg}}$$

$$mass\ in\ g = 35,000\ g$$

Prefix	Symbol	Meaning	Multiple of base unit
mega-	M	million	1,000,000
kilo-	k	thousand	1,000
deci-	d	tenth	0.1
centi-	c	hundredth	0.01
milli-	m	thousandth	0.001
micro-	μ	millionth	0.000001

PRACTICE

1. On March 24, 1989, the *Exxon Valdez* struck a reef in Prince William Sound, Alaska, spilling 37,854,120 L of crude oil. What is this volume in milliliters?

| Math Skills *continued* |

2. The Tent meteorite, found in 1897 near Cape York, on the west coast of Greenland, is the largest meteorite exhibited by any museum. It has a mass of 30,883 kg. How much is the mass of this meteorite in milligrams?

3. Speed skater Kim Ki-hoon, of South Korea, won the 1,000 m short-track race in the 1992 Olympics with a time of 90.76 s. How many milliseconds did it take him to finish the race? How many centimeters long was the race?

PROBLEM

At 553 m tall, the CN Tower, in Toronto, Canada, is one of the tallest structures in the world. What is the tower's height in kilometers?

SOLUTION

Step 1: List the given and unknown values.

   Given: *height in meters* = 553 m

   Unknown: *height in kilometers* = ? km

Step 2: Determine the relationship between units. Using the table on the previous page, you can see that 1,000 m = 1 km. You will divide because there are fewer kilometers than meters in a given distance.

Step 3: Write the equation for the conversion.

$$height\ in\ km = height\ in\ m \times \frac{1\ km}{1,000\ m}$$

Step 4: Insert the known values into the equation, and solve.

$$height\ in\ km = 553\ \cancel{m} \times \frac{1\ km}{1,000\ \cancel{m}}$$

$$height\ in\ km = 0.553\ km$$

PRACTICE

4. One of the smallest species of insects in the world is *Caraphractus cinctus,* a type of wasp. The average mass of this wasp is 5 μg. Convert this mass into grams.

5. Scientists studying bull sperm whales off the coast of South Africa have calculated that these mammals can descend to depths of nearly 3,000 m during their search for food. What is this depth in kilometers?

6. Laura runs a 100 m race in 20.0 s. What is her time in kiloseconds? How long is the race in kilometers?

_____

7. It does not take a large electric current, the amount of charge that passes through a substance each second, to cause a fatal shock. The smallest deadly amount of electricity through the human body is 100 mA (milliamperes). What is this current in amperes?

_____

8. Pikes Peak is a mountain in Colorado. Its height is 4,301 m above sea level. What is this altitude in kilometers?

_____

9. Yosemite Falls, in California, has a total height of 73,900 cm. What is this height in meters?

_____

10. The Rio Grande is the river between Texas and Mexico, but not everyone realizes that it begins in Colorado and flows through New Mexico. The river's total length is 3,033,000 m. How many kilometers is this?

_____

PROBLEM

There are 60 minutes in an hour. What is this amount of time in seconds?

SOLUTION

Step 1: **List the given and unknown values.**

> **Given:** *time in minutes* = 60 min

> **Unknown:** *time in seconds* = ? s

Step 2: **Determine the relationship between units.** Although minutes do not fit strictly in the SI system, they can be used with it. Note that there are 60 seconds in a minute. You will multiply because there are many seconds in each minute.

Step 3: **Write the equation for the conversion.**

$$time\ in\ s = time\ in\ min \times \frac{60\ s}{1\ min}$$

Step 4: **Insert the known values into the equation, and solve.**

$$time\ in\ s = 60\ \cancel{min} \times \frac{60\ s}{1\ \cancel{min}}$$

$$time\ in\ s = 3,600\ s$$

PRACTICE

11. The purpose of the sport called *flight archery* is to shoot an arrow the greatest possible distance. One of the greatest distances achieved in flight archery is 624 m. What would this distance be in centimeters?

_____

12. The French drink about 64 L of mineral water per person per year. How many milliliters does each person drink annually? How much mineral water, in milliliters, does each person drink each month?

_____

13. In the United States' electrical system, the electric current in a 75 watt light bulb is 6,250 mA. What is this current in amperes?

_____

14. An acre is a common unit used to measure the area of a portion of land. An acre is equal to about 4,046.9 m^2. What is this area in square kilometers (km^2)? (**Hint:** Because 1 km is equal to 1,000 m, 1 $km^2 = (1,000)^2$ $m^2 = 1,000,000$ m^2.)

_____

15. One of the smallest nations in the world is Liechtenstein, a tiny country between Switzerland and Austria in Europe. If its area is 160 km^2, how many square meters is this area?

_____

16. The largest planet in the solar system is Jupiter, with a diameter of 71,398 km. What is the diameter of Jupiter in centimeters?

_____

Skills Worksheet

Math Skills

Writing Scientific Notation

After you study each sample problem and solution, work out the practice problems on a separate sheet of paper. Write your answers in the spaces provided.

PROBLEM

A single railroad engine pulled 250 freight cars on the Erie Railroad from May 1914 until 1929. The mass pulled by the engine was 15,545,000 kg. Express this value for mass in scientific notation.

SOLUTION

Step 1:   List the given value.

   Given: *mass, m* = 15,545,000 kg

Step 2:   Write the form for scientific notation.

$$m = ? \times 10^? \text{ kg}$$

Step 3: Convert the known value into the form for scientific notation. Move the decimal point to the left until only one digit remains to the left of the decimal point. Count the number of places the decimal point was moved. To change 15,545,000 to 1.554 5000, the decimal point is moved seven places to the left. The number of places the decimal point is moved is the correct power of 10. When the decimal point is moved to the left, the exponent is positive. The zeros at the end of the number can be dropped from the answer.

$$m = 1.5545 \times 10^7 \text{ kg}$$

PRACTICE

1. Scientists have estimated that the area of Earth covered by water is 70.98 percent, or 362,031,100 km^2. Express this value in scientific notation.

_____

2. The brightest comet on record, the Great Comet of 1843, had a tail that trailed for 205,000,000 mi. Express this distance in scientific notation.

_____

3. Mount Everest, an eastern Himalayan peak on the Tibet-Nepal border, was discovered to be the world's highest mountain in March 1856. The Survey Department of the Government of India computed its height to be 29,002 ft. Express this height in scientific notation.

_____

4. The Great Barrier Reef, off Queensland, northeastern Australia, is actually not a single reef but consists of thousands of separate reefs. Together, they stretch for a length of 2,027,773 m. Express this distance in scientific notation.

_____

5. The material cost of World War II has been estimated at $1.5 trillion. In May 1959, the total cost to the Soviet Union was estimated at 2,500,000,000,000 rubles. Express this monetary value in scientific notation.

_____

6. The speed of light in outer space is about 300,000,000 m/s. Express this speed in scientific notation.

_____

PROBLEM

The diameter of the hydrogen atom has been measured to be about 0.00000001 m. Express this diameter in scientific notation.

SOLUTION

Step 1:   List the given value.

   Given: *diameter, d* = 0.00000001 m

Step 2:   Write the form for scientific notation.

   $$d = ? \times 10^? \text{ m}$$

Step 3:   Convert the known value into the form for scientific notation. Move the decimal point to the right until the first nonzero digit is to the left of the decimal point. Count the number of places the decimal point was moved. To change 0.000 00001 to 1.0, the decimal point is moved eight places to the right. The number of places the decimal point is moved is the correct power of 10. When the decimal point is moved to the right, the exponent is negative.

   $$d = 1.0 \times 10^{-8} \text{ m}$$

PRACTICE

7. In 1981 the IBM Zurich research laboratory invented the scanning tunneling microscope (STM). It has a magnifying ability of 100 million with resolution capability down to 0.0000000002 m, about the diameter of a sulfur atom. Express the value 0.0000000002 m in scientific notation.

_____

Math Skills *continued*

8. One of the smallest of all free-living organisms, *Mycoplasma laidlawii,* was first discovered in sewage in 1936. During its early existence, its diameter can be as small as only 0.0000001 m. Express this diameter in scientific notation.

_____

9. The mass of the smallest bacterium is about 0.0000000000000002 g. Express this value in scientific notation.

_____

10. The speed with which the shutter of a camera opens and shuts can be changed on certain models of cameras. On most 35 mm cameras, the fastest shutter speed is 0.001 s. Express this time in scientific notation.

_____

11. Although you cannot see it, the lights in a room flicker on and off several times a second. The flickering results from the electricity changing direction rapidly, causing the lights to brighten and dim repeatedly. This cycle occurs once every 0.0166 s. Express this time interval in scientific notation.

_____

12. The density of helium is 0.000178 g/cm^3. Express helium's density using scientific notation.

_____

Skills Worksheet

Math Skills

Using Scientific Notation

After you study each sample problem and solution, work out the practice problems on a separate sheet of paper. Write your answers in the spaces provided.

PROBLEM

The Concorde, a supersonic passenger jet that flies from the East Coast of the United States to London and Paris, must fly at the speed of a regular jet while flying over land. This lower speed is used to avoid problems associated with the sonic boom of supersonic jets. Once over the Atlantic Ocean, the Concorde can increase its speed. If the Concorde flies at 8.85×10^2 km/h over land and 2.300×10^3 km/h over sea, what is the difference in these speeds?

SOLUTION

Step 1: **List the given and unknown values.**

Given: *land speed* $= 8.85 \times 10^2$ km/h

sea speed $= 2.300 \times 10^3$ km/h

Unknown: *difference in speeds* $= ?$ km/h

Step 2: **Write the equation for the difference in speeds.**

Difference in speeds = sea speed – land speed

Step 3: **Insert the known values into the equation, and solve.**

Difference in speeds $= (2.300 \times 10^3$ km/h$) - (8.85 \times 10^2$ km/h$)$

Rewrite either value so that the exponent term of both numbers is the same.

2.300×10^3 km/h $= 23.00 \times 10^2$ km/h

Difference in speeds $= (23.00 - 8.85) \times 10^2$ km/h

Difference in speeds $= 14.15 \times 10^2$ km/h

Rewrite the value with only one nonzero digit to the left of the decimal point.

Difference in speeds $= 1.415 \times 10^3$ km/h

PRACTICE

1. The heaviest commonly used United States coin is the half dollar, which has a mass of 11.340 g. The lightest United States coin is the dime, which has a mass of 2.268 g. Report the sum of these masses in scientific notation.

2. A signal is transmitted between four microwave signal towers. The distances between the towers is 2.50 km, 2.500×10^1 km, and 5.0×10^{-1} km. What is the total distance traveled by the signal?

_____

3. The adult house fly lives for only about 1 month, or 8×10^{-2} y. The oldest recorded age of a tortoise was 1.8800×10^2 y. What is the difference between these two ages?

_____

4. The ink needed to dot an *i* in this book has a mass of around 0.000000001 kg. What is the mass of ink needed to dot all of the *i*'s in this problem?

_____

PROBLEM

The Friends of St. Catherine's Hospice, from Crawley, United Kingdom, made a blanket that measured 4.5×10^3 cm by 7.7×10^3 cm. It was later split into more than 1,450 smaller blankets, which were donated to charity. What was the overall area of the original blanket in square centimeters (cm^2)?

SOLUTION

Step 1:   List the given and unknown values.

  Given: *length, l* $= 4.5 \times 10^3$ cm

  width, w $= 7.7 \times 10^3$ cm

 Unknown: *area, A* $= ?$ cm^2

Step 2:   Write the equation for area.

  $A = l \times w$

Step 3:   Insert the known values into the equation, and solve.

  $A = (4.5 \times 10^3 \text{ cm})(7.7 \times 10^3 \text{ cm})$

Regroup the values and units as follows.

  $A = (4.5 \times 7.7)(10^3 \times 10^3)(\text{cm} \times \text{cm})$

When multiplying, add the powers of 10.

  $A = (4.5 \times 7.7)(10^{3+3})(\text{cm} \times \text{cm})$

  $A = 35 \times 10^6 \text{ cm}^2$

  $A = 3.5 \times 10^7 \text{ cm}^2$

PRACTICE

5. The Republic of China presented one of the world's largest flags to the city of Kaohsiung in 1989. The flag of the Republic of China measured 1.26×10^4 cm by 8.40×10^3 cm. What is the area of this flag in square centimeters?

_____

6. Certain large cardboard boxes are manufactured by a packaging plant for an appliance outlet store. Each box has dimensions of $1.88 \times 1.65 \times 1.25$ m. What is the volume of the box in cubic centimeters (cm^3)?

_____

7. One of the greatest meteor showers ever recorded occurred on the night of November 17, 1966. The Leonid meteors, so called because they appear to originate in the constellation Leo, were visible from western North America to eastern Russia. Scientists calculated that meteors passed over Arizona at a rate of 1.38×10^5 per hour for 3.33×10^{-1} hours. Calculate how many meteors passed over Arizona that night.

_____

8. The moon is Earth's closest neighbor and its only natural satellite. The moon has an average orbital speed of 1.03×10^3 m/s. If the mass of the moon is 7.35×10^{22} kg, calculate its momentum using the equation *momentum = mass × speed.*

_____

PROBLEM

Gold, one of the densest elements, is so dense that 1.0 cm^3 of the element has a mass of 1.93×10^1 g. If you have a sample of gold with a mass of 2.54×10^2 g, what is its volume?

SOLUTION

Step 1: **List the given and unknown values.**

Given: *mass, m* $= 2.54 \times 10^2$ g

density, D $= 1.93 \times 10^1$ g/cm³

Unknown: *volume, V* $= ?$ cm³

Step 2: **Write the equation for volume.**

$V = m/D$

Step 3: **Insert the known values into the equation, and solve.**

$$V = \frac{2.54 \times 10^2 \text{ g}}{1.93 \times 10^1 \text{ g/cm}^3}$$

Regroup the values and units as follows:

$$V = \left(\frac{2.54}{1.93}\right)\left(\frac{10^2}{10^1}\right)\left(\frac{g}{g/cm^3}\right)$$

When dividing, subtract the denominator's power of 10 from the numerator's power of 10.

$$V = \left(\frac{2.54}{1.93}\right) \times \left(\frac{10^{2-1}}{1}\right)\left(\frac{g}{g/cm^3}\right)$$

$$V = 1.32 \times 10^1 \ cm^3$$

PRACTICE

9. Use the equation *speed = distance/time* to find the speed of a freight train that travels 3.7×10^6 m in 3.13×10^5 s.

_____

10. On November 1, 1965, the first high-speed Japanese bullet trains, called *Shinkansen,* provided regular scheduled service at speeds averaging over 45 m/s. Calculate the average speed of a *Shinkansen* that traveled between the Japanese cities of Tokyo and Osaka, a distance of 5.17×10^5 m, in 1.14×10^4 s.

_____

11. One of the longest nonstop delivery flights by a commercial jet occurred August 16–17, 1989, when a Boeing 747-400 jet flew 1.81×10^7 m from London, England, to Sydney, Australia. The average speed of the jet was 2.49×10^2 m/s. Calculate how long it took this commercial airliner to reach its destination, using the equation *time = distance/speed.*

_____

12. Any long piece of wire, rope, or cable that is made of an unchanging substance and has a uniform thickness is said to have a constant linear density. Linear density is measured in units of mass per unit length. Suppose you have a copper wire that has a linear density of 1.75×10^2 g/m. If the mass of the wire is 4.85×10^3 g, how long is the wire? (**Hint:** Use the equation *length = mass/linear density.*)

_____

Skills Worksheet

Math Skills

Using Significant Figures

After you study each sample problem and solution, work out the practice problems on a separate sheet of paper. Write your answers in the spaces provided.

PROBLEM

The approximate volumes of the Great Lakes are as follows: 4.5×10^{11} m³ for Lake Erie, 1.6×10^{12} m³ for Lake Ontario, 4.5×10^{12} m³ for Lake Huron, 5.4×10^{12} m³ for Lake Michigan, and 1.1×10^{13} m³ for Lake Superior. Calculate the total volume of water in the Great Lakes, and write the answer using the correct number of significant figures.

SOLUTION

Step 1: List the given and unknown values.

Given: *volume of Lake Erie, $V_1 = 4.5 \times 10^{11}$ m³*
volume of Lake Ontario, $V_2 = 1.6 \times 10^{12}$ m³
volume of Lake Huron, $V_3 = 4.5 \times 10^{12}$ m³
volume of Lake Michigan, $V_4 = 5.4 \times 10^{12}$ m³
volume of Lake Superior, $V_5 = 1.1 \times 10^{13}$ m³

Unknown: *total volume of Great Lakes, $V = ?$ m³*

Step 2: Write the equation for the total volume.

$$V = V_1 + V_2 + V_3 + V_4 + V_5$$

Step 3: Insert the known values into the equation, and solve.

$$V = (4.5 \times 10^{11} \text{ m}^3) + (1.6 \times 10^{12} \text{ m}^3) + (4.5 \times 10^{12} \text{ m}^3) + (5.4 \times 10^{12} \text{ m}^3) + (1.1 \times 10^{13} \text{ m}^3)$$

$$V = (0.045 + 0.16 + 0.45 + 0.54 + 1.1) \times 10^{13} \text{ m}^3$$

$$V = 2.295 \times 10^{13} \text{ m}^3$$

The answer should have only one significant figure to the right of the decimal point because the number with the smallest number of significant figures has only one number to the right of the decimal point.

$$V = 2.3 \times 10^{13} \text{ m}^3$$

PRACTICE

1. A roadside picnic area is located at the 1,453 km marker of a highway. The next picnic area is at the 1,615 km marker. Calculate the distance between the two areas, and write the answer with the correct number of significant figures.

2. Venus comes closer to Earth than any other planet: 4.02×10^7 km. By contrast, the closest the outer planet Neptune ever comes to Earth is 4.35×10^9 km. Calculate the difference between these two distances, and write the answer with the correct number of significant figures.

_____

3. Three properties with areas of 20.34 km^2, 18.0 km^2, and 25.333 km^2 are for sale. Calculate the total area of the properties, and write the answer using the correct number of significant figures.

_____

PROBLEM

A small airtight room is filled with CO_2 gas to conduct an experiment. The room is 2.75 m high, 1.685 m wide, and 3.25 m long. Calculate the volume of the room into which the CO_2 gas is dispersed. Write the answer with the correct number of significant figures.

SOLUTION

Step 1:   List the given and unknown values.

  Given: *length, l* = 3.25m

          width, w = 1.685 m

          height, h = 2.75 m

  Unknown: *Volume, V* = ?

Step 2:   Write the equation for volume.

          Volume, $V = l \times w \times h$

Step 3:   Insert the known values into the equation, and solve.

          $V = 3.25 \text{ m} \times 1.685 \text{ m} \times 2.75 \text{ m}$

          $V = 15.0596875 \text{ m}^3$

The answer should have three significant figures because the value with the smallest number of significant figures has three significant figures.

          $V = 15.1 \text{ m}^3$

PRACTICE

4. A small roll of double-sided tape is 6.35 m long and 1.2×10^{-2} m wide. What is the total area that could be covered by this roll of tape? Write the answer with the correct number of significant figures.

_____

5. Calculate the volume of a rectangular swimming pool that is 20.46 m × 12.475 m × 2.25 m. Write the answer with the correct number of significant figures.

_____

6. The dimensions of a new store's "Grand Opening" banner are 7.62 m × 3.6576 m. Calculate the area of the rectangular banner, and write the answer with the correct number of significant figures.

_____

7. A rectangular clear-plastic container is filled with nickels at a carnival booth. The container is 45.675 cm tall, 18.75 cm wide, and 9.325 cm long. Calculate the volume of the container, and write the answer using the correct number of significant figures.

_____

8. A high school football team practices on a field that is 73.152 m long × 30.1752 m wide. Calculate the area of the field, and write the answer with the correct number of significant figures.

_____

PROBLEM

A satellite orbits Earth 500 km above Earth's surface. If the satellite travels 252 km in 33 s, what is its speed? Write the answer with the correct number of significant figures.

SOLUTION

Step 1: List the given and unknown values.

Given: *distance, d* = 252 km

time, t = 33 s

Unknown: *speed, v* = ? km/s

Step 2: Write the equation for speed.

$$speed, v = \frac{d}{t}$$

Step 3: Insert the values into the equation, and solve.

$$v = \frac{252 \text{ km}}{33 \text{ s}}$$

$$v = 7.636 \text{ km/s}$$

The answer should have two significant figures because the value with the smallest number of significant figures has two numbers.

$$v = 7.6 \text{ km/s}$$

Math Skills *continued*

PRACTICE

9. On May 5, 1979, Dr. Hans Liebold achieved one of the highest average lap speeds on any closed-circuit racetrack. Racing in a Mercedes-Benz C111-IV experimental coupe in Nardo, Italy, Liebold lapped the 12,633.35 m high-speed track in 112.67 s. Calculate his average lap speed, and write the answer with the correct number of significant figures.

_____

10. In 1973, Secretariat was the winning horse in the Kentucky Derby, at Churchill Downs, in Louisville, Kentucky. Secretariat ran 2,011.68 m in 119.4 s. Calculate the average speed of the horse, and write the answer with the correct number of significant figures.

_____

11. On October 3–5, 1931, Major Clyde Pangborn and Hugh Herndon navigated the first nonstop trans-Pacific flight, in the Bellanca cabin monoplane *Miss Veedol.* They flew 7,335,389.952 m, from Sabishiro Beach, Japan, to Wenatchee, Washington, in 148,380 s. Calculate their average speed, and write the answer with the correct number of significant figures.

_____

12. Seppo-Juhani Savolainen cross-country skied 415,532.6 m in 24 hours (86,400 s) in Saariselka, Finland, on April 8–9, 1988. Calculate the average speed of the skier, and write the answer with the correct number of significant figures.

_____

Skills Worksheet

Math Skills

Density

After you study each sample problem and solution, work out the practice problems on a separate sheet of paper. Write your answers in the spaces provided.

PROBLEM

The largest meteorite discovered on Earth is the Hoba West stone in Namibia, Africa. The volume of the stone is about 7.5 m³. If the meteorite has a density of 8.0 g/cm³, what is its mass?

SOLUTION

Step 1: **List the given and the unknown values.**

> **Given:** *volume, V* = 7.5 m³
>
> *density, D* = 8.0 g/cm³
>
> **Unknown:** *mass, m* = ? kg

Step 2: **Rearrange the density equation to calculate for mass.**

$$density = \frac{mass}{volume}$$

$$mass = density \times volume$$

$$m = D \times V$$

Step 3: **Insert the known values into the equation, and solve.**

$$m = \left(\frac{8.0 \text{ g}}{\text{cm}^3} \times \frac{10^6 \text{ cm}^3}{\text{m}^3}\right) \times 7.5 \text{ m}^3 = 6.0 \times 10^7 \text{ g}$$

$$m = 6.0 \times 10^{4 \text{ kg}}$$

PRACTICE

1. The largest ruby in the world is 10.9 cm long, 9.10 cm wide, and 5.80 cm thick, giving it an overall volume of 575 cm³. If the density of ruby—a form of aluminum oxide—is 3.97 g/cm³, what is the mass of the largest ruby?

_____

2. Certain compounds called *aerogels* form rigid, lightweight foams that can support a mass many times greater than their own. If a sample of an aerogel has a volume of 87.3 cm³ and a density of 0.250 g/cm³, what is its mass?

_____

3. Osmium, a hard, heavy metal used to make durable alloys, has a density of 22.5 g/cm^3, the greatest density of any element. If a sample of osmium has a volume of 43.2 cm^3, what is its mass?

_____

4. The element iridium is more resistant to corrosion than any other metal. It also has a slightly smaller density than osmium: 22.42 g/cm^3. Suppose you have a sample of iridium with a volume of 34.17 cm^3. What is the mass of this sample?

_____

5. A neutron star, which is the remnant of an exploded massive star, consists of neutrons packed together with a total density of 3.03×10^{14} g/cm^3. If you had a 1.40 cm^3 sample of this matter (about the size of a sugar cube), what would its mass be?

_____

PROBLEM

One of the largest emeralds ever discovered had a mass of 17.23 kg. Assuming its density to be 4.02 g/cm^3, what was the emerald's volume?

SOLUTION

Step 1: **List the given and the unknown values.**

Given: *mass, m* = 17.23 kg

density, D = 4.02 g/cm^3

Unknown: *volume, V* = ? cm^3

Step 2: **Rearrange the density equation to calculate for volume.**

$$density = \frac{mass}{volume}$$

$$volume = \frac{mass}{density}$$

$$V = \frac{m}{D}$$

Step 3: **Insert the known values into the equation, and solve.**

$$V = \frac{17.23 \text{ kg}}{4.02 \text{ g/cm}^3} \times \frac{10^3 \text{ g}}{\text{kg}}$$

$$V = 4.29 \times 10^3 \text{ cm}^3$$

PRACTICE

6. Magnesium is a fairly light metal that is combined with other elements to form lightweight alloys for use in airplanes. The big advantage of magnesium is that it has a relatively low density of 1.74 g/cm³. If a sample of magnesium has a mass of 9.56 g, what is its volume?

_____

7. Moon rocks are samples of the moon's crust that were collected and returned to Earth by crew members of the various Apollo missions. Many of the moon rocks are made of basalt, a light, volcanic rock with a density of about 2.7 g/cm³. If a moon rock has a mass of 432 g, what is its volume?

_____

8. Although both diamond and graphite consist of pure carbon, they have very different densities because of differences in the way the carbon atoms in each substance are arranged. If you had a diamond with a mass of 1.5 g and a density of 3.51 g/cm³, what would its volume be?

_____

9. One of the largest gold nuggets ever discovered was found in Australia in 1872. The nugget had a mass of 286 kg. Given that 19.32 g/cm³ is the density of gold, calculate the volume of this nugget.

_____

10. Gasoline, which is a mixture of several hydrocarbon compounds, has one of the lowest densities of any liquid. Given that 0.70 g/cm³ is the density of gasoline, determine the volume of 2.77 kg of gasoline.

_____

PROBLEM

Lithium is the lightest of metals and the least dense of all nongaseous elements. A pure lithium sample with a volume of 13.0 cm³ has a mass of 6.94 g. What is the density of lithium?

SOLUTION

Step 1:   List the given and the unknown values.

Given: *mass, m* = 6.94 g

volume, V = 13.0 cm³

Unknown: *density, D* = ? g/cm³

| Math Skills *continued*

Step 2: **Write equation for density.**

$$density = \frac{mass}{volume} \qquad D = \frac{m}{V}$$

Step 3: **Insert the known values into the equation, and solve.**

$$D = \frac{m}{V} = \frac{6.94 \text{ g}}{13.0 \text{ cm}^3}$$

$$D = 0.534 \text{ g/cm}^3$$

PRACTICE

11. Outer space is often described as a vacuum, but there is always some matter present. In the space 300 km above Earth's surface, there is as little as 1.58×10^{-12} g of matter in a 500.0 cm³ volume of space. Based on this data, what is the density of the matter in space?

_____

12. The volume of a liquid that fills a flask is 750 cm³. The mass of the liquid is 525 g. What is the liquid's density? Is it most likely to be water ($D = 1.0$ g/cm³), gasoline ($D = 0.70$ g/cm³), or ethanol ($D = 0.79$ g/cm³)?

_____

MIXED PRACTICE

13. Because inland seas like the Caspian Sea or the Great Salt Lake evaporate faster than they can be refilled, they have higher concentrations of salts than oceans have. The highest concentration of salts in any body of water is found in the Dead Sea, in Israel. If you had 1,230 cm³ of this water, which has a density of 1.22 g/cm³, what would be its mass?

_____

14. *Density 21.5* is the title of a composition written for a musician with a platinum flute. Platinum's density is closer to 21.45 g/cm³. If the platinum flute's mass is 2.000 kg, what is its volume?

_____

15. The density of seawater is slightly higher than that of fresh water. The higher density is due to the fact that seawater contains salts such as sodium chloride and magnesium chloride. Suppose you have a container that holds 5.00 kg of fresh water, which has a density of 1.00 g/cm³. If 5.00 kg of seawater with a density of 1.03 g/cm³ is placed in a container of the same size, what is the volume of the space that is left unfilled?

_____

Skills Worksheet

Math Skills

Pascal's Principle

After you study each sample problem and solution, work out the practice problems on a separate sheet of paper. Write your answers in the spaces provided.

PROBLEM

A dentist's chair makes use of Pascal's principle to move patients up and down. Together, the chair and a patient exert a downward force of 2,269 N. The chair is attached to a large piston with an area of 1,221 cm^2. To move the chair, a pump applies force to a small piston with an area of 88.12 cm^2. What force must be exerted on the small piston to lift the chair?

SOLUTION

Step 1: List the given and unknown values.

Given: $F_2 = 2,269$ N

$A_1 = 88.12$ cm^2

$A_2 = 1,221$ cm^2

Unknown: F_1

Step 2: Write the equations for Pascal's principle and pressure, force, and area.

$$p_1 = p_2$$

$$pressure = \frac{force}{area}$$

Step 3: Substitute force and area into the first equation, and rearrange for the desired value.

$$p_1 = p_2$$

$$\frac{F_1}{A_1} = \frac{F_2}{A_2}$$

$$F_1 = \frac{(F_2)(A_1)}{A_2}$$

Step 4: Insert the known values into the equation, and solve.

$$F_1 = \frac{(2269 \text{ N})(88.12 \text{ cm}^2)}{1221 \text{ cm}^2}$$

$$F_1 = 163.8 \text{ N}$$

PRACTICE

1. A hydraulic lift office chair has its seat attached to a piston with an area of 11.2 cm^2. The chair is raised by exerting force on another piston, with an area of 4.12 cm^2. If a person sitting on the chair exerts a downward force of 219 N, what force needs to be exerted on the small piston to lift the seat?

_____

2. In changing a tire, a hydraulic jack lifts 7,468 N on its large piston, which has an area of 28.27 cm^2. How much force must be exerted on the small piston if it has an area of 1.325 cm^2?

_____

3. An engine shop uses a lift to raise a 1,784 N engine. The lift has a large piston with an area of 76.32 cm^2. To raise the lift, force is exerted on a small piston with an area of 12.56 cm^2. What force must be exerted to raise the lift?

_____

PROBLEM

An engineering student wants to build a hydraulic pump to lift a 1,815 N crate. The pump will have two pistons connected via a fluid chamber. The student calculates that a force of 442 N will be exerted on the small piston, which will have an area of 50.2 cm^2. What must the area of the large piston be to exert the desired force?

SOLUTION

Step 1: **List the given and unknown values.**

Given: $F_1 = 442$ N

$A_1 = 50.2$ cm^2

$F_2 = 1,815$ N

Unknown: A_2

Step 2: **Write the equations for Pascal's principle and pressure, force, and area.**

$$p_1 = p_2$$

$$pressure = \frac{force}{area}$$

Step 3: **Substitute force and area into the first equation, and rearrange for the desired value.**

$$p_1 = p_2$$

$$\frac{F_1}{A_1} = \frac{F_2}{A_2}$$

$$A_2 = \frac{F_2(A_1)}{F_1}$$

| Math Skills *continued*

Step 4:   Insert the known values into the equation, and solve.

$$A_2 = \frac{(1815 \text{ N})(50.2 \text{ cm}^2)}{442 \text{ N}}$$

$$A_2 = 206 \text{ cm}^2$$

PRACTICE

4. In a newly designed car with a hydraulic braking system, a force of 85 N is applied to one of the master cylinders, which has an area of 8.1 cm². The master cylinder is connected to one brake piston, which exerts a force of 296 N. What is the area of the brake piston?

_____

5. A mechanic uses a hydraulic car jack to lift the front end of a car to change the oil. The jack used exerts 8,915 N of force from the larger piston. To pump the jack, 444 N of force is exerted on the small piston, which has an area of 3.14 cm². What is the area of the large piston?

_____

6. A student in the lunchroom blows into his straw with a force of 0.26 N. The column of air pushing the liquid in the glass has an area of 0.21 cm². If the liquid in the glass pushes upward with a force of 79 N, what is the area of the liquid at the surface of the glass?

_____

PROBLEM

The motor on a construction-grade hydraulic shovel exerts 3.11×10^7 Pa of pressure on a fluid tank. The fluid tank is connected to a piston that has an area of 153 cm². How much force does the piston exert?

SOLUTION

Step 1:   List the given and unknown values.

Given: $p_1 = 3.11 \times 10^7$ Pa

$A_2 = 153 \text{ cm}^2$

Unknown: F_2

Step 2:   Write the equations for Pascal's principle and pressure, force, and area.

$$p_1 = p_2$$

$$pressure = \frac{force}{area}$$

Step 3: **Substitute force and area into the first equation, and rearrange for the desired value.**

$$p_1 = p_2$$
$$p_1 = \frac{F_2}{A_2}$$
$$F_2 = (p_1)(A_2)$$

Step 4: **Insert the known values into the equation, and solve.**

$$F_2 = (3.11 \times 10^7 \, \text{Pa})(153 \, \text{cm}^2)$$
$$F_2 = \left(\frac{3.11 \times 10^7 \, \text{N}}{\text{m}^2}\right)(1.53 \times 10^{-2} \, \text{m}^2)$$
$$F_2 = 4.76 \times 10^5 \, \text{N}$$

PRACTICE

7. A small crane has a motor that exerts 2.41×10^7 of pressure on a fluid chamber. The chamber is connected by a fluid line to a piston on the crane arm. If the piston has an area of 168 cm^2, how much force does the piston exert?

_____

8. A bicycle pump uses Pascal's law to operate. The air in the hose acts as a fluid and transfers force and pressure from the piston to the tire. If a pump has a piston with an area of 7.1 cm^2, how much force must be exerted on it to create a pressure of 8.2×10^5 Pa?

_____

9. A small backyard log splitter has an engine that applies 1.723×10^7 of pressure to a fluid tank. The tank is connected to a piston with an area of 81.07 cm^2. How much force can the piston exert?

_____

MIXED PRACTICE

10. A force of 38.7 N is applied to the master cylinder of a hydraulic brake system. The cylinder has an area of 7.61 cm^2. The force from the master cylinder is transferred, by brake fluid, to two brake cylinders that have a total area of 49.1 cm^2. How much total force is exerted by the brake cylinders?

_____

11. A factory lift is used to raise a load of 2,225 N on a piston that has an area of 706.8 cm^2. How much pressure does the lift's engine need to exert on the hydraulic fluid to lift the required load?

_____

Skills Worksheet

Math Skills

Boyle's Law

After you study each sample problem and solution, work out the practice problems on a separate sheet of paper. Write your answers in the spaces provided.

PROBLEM

To make an air horn, 1.50 L of air at 101 kPa are compressed into a can with a volume of 0.462 L. Assuming a constant temperature, what is the pressure on the compressed air?

SOLUTION

Step 1: List the given and unknown values.

> **Given:** $V_1 = 1.50$ L
>
> $P_1 = 101$ kPa
>
> $V_2 = 0.462$ L
>
> **Unknown:** P_2

Step 2: Write the equation for Boyle's law, then rearrange the equation to isolate the value you want to find.

$$P_1V_1 = P_2V_2$$
$$P_2 = \frac{P_1V_1}{V_2}$$

Step 3: Substitute the known values into the equation, and solve.

$$P_2 = \frac{(101 \text{ kPa})(1.50 \text{ L})}{(0.462 \text{ L})}$$
$$P_2 = 328 \text{ kPa}$$

PRACTICE

1. A science class puts a balloon containing 1.25 L of air at 101 kPa into a bell jar. Using an air pump, the class removes some of the air in the jar, causing the balloon to expand to a volume of 2.25 L. Assuming a constant temperature, what is the new pressure inside the jar?

_____

2. A small balloon is inflated with helium at 102 kPa to a volume of 2.12 L. According to the balloon's manufacturer, if the balloon is stretched to a volume of 4.25 L, the balloon will pop. If the balloon were released, at what pressure would the balloon pop? Assume constant temperature throughout.

_____

3. An oxygen supplier wants to reduce the volume of her oxygen tanks. She plans to take the oxygen in her 155 L tanks and store it in 95.5 L tanks. If the oxygen in the old tanks has a pressure of 8.27×10^3 kPa, what will the new pressure be after the oxygen is compressed? Assume a constant temperature throughout.

4. A blocked bicycle pump contains 0.682 L of air at 99.3 kPa. If the handle is pressed down, decreasing the volume of the inside air to 0.151 L, what is the pressure inside the pump? Assume that the temperature of the air does not change.

PROBLEM

A balloon is filled with air at a pressure of 105 kPa. Then the pressure around the balloon is increased to 205 kPa. If the balloon originally had a volume of 4.11 L, what is the new volume of the balloon? Assume constant temperature throughout.

SOLUTION

Step 1:   List the given and unknown values.

Given: $V_1 = 4.11$ L

$P_1 = 105$ kPa

$P_2 = 205$ kPa

Unknown: V_2

Step 2:   Write the equation for Boyle's law, then rearrange the equation to isolate the value you want to find.

$$P_1V_1 = P_2V_2$$
$$V_2 = \frac{P_1V_1}{P_2}$$

Step 3:   Substitute the known values into the equation, and solve.

$$V_2 = \frac{(105 \text{ kPa})(4.11 \text{ L})}{205 \text{ kPa}}$$
$$V_2 = 2.11 \text{ L}$$

PRACTICE

5. An oxygen tank holds 355 L of oxygen at 8.23×10^3 kPa. What volume would the same amount of oxygen take up if the pressure were reduced to 4.11×10^3 kPa ? Assume that the temperature remains the same.

6. A machine produces 599 L of hydrogen at 101 kPa each day. If each day's supply of hydrogen were kept at a pressure of 366 kPa, what would be the volume of the hydrogen? Assume that temperature is constant throughout.

_____

7. A diver's tank holds 15.1 L of air at a pressure of 1.53×10^4 kPa. If the air was released underwater at a pressure of 6.11×10^2 kPa, what would the volume of the released air be? Assume that temperature remains constant throughout.

_____

8. A plastic food storage bag is sealed with 0.213 L of air inside at a pressure of 99.2 kPa. The bag is loaded onto a plane, where the pressure is decreased to 80.5 kPa. What is the size of the air in the bag after the pressure is decreased, if the temperature of the air remains the same?

_____

MIXED PRACTICE

9. A balloon is filled with helium in an airplane, where the air pressure is 81 kPa. The filled balloon has a volume of 4.2 L. When the plane lands, the cabin is depressurized to the outside air pressure, which is 94 kPa. If the temperature of the balloon remains the same, what is the new volume of the balloon?

_____

10. A small helium tank claims to be able to fill 30 balloons to a volume of 3.15 L at a pressure of 101 kPa. How many liters of helium will the tank be able to produce at a pressure of 94.2 kPa? Assume that the temperature of the tank remains the same throughout.

_____

11. A scuba diver carries a small balloon of air deep underwater. If the balloon has a volume of 2.11 L at the surface, where the pressure is 102 kPa, what will the pressure be when the balloon has shrunk to a size of 0.581 L? Assume that the balloon's temperature remains the same throughout its descent.

_____

12. A medical supply company stores oxygen in a 200.5 L tank at a pressure of 9,585 kPa. If the company transfers all of the oxygen to a 350.8 L tank, what will the pressure be inside the tank, if the temperature stays the same?

_____

13. At a sewage treatment plant, methane is gathered for energy use. If 75 L of methane is produced at 94 kPa, how many liters would be produced at 100 kPa? Assume temperature remains constant throughout.

_____

Skills Worksheet

Math Skills

Conversion Factors

After you study each sample problem and solution, work out the practice problems on a separate sheet of paper. Write your answers in the spaces provided.

PROBLEM

A flight from Chicago to New York costs $0.240/km. If the distance between the two cities is 1,075 km, what is the total cost of the flight?

SOLUTION

Step 1: **List the given and unknown values.**

> **Given:** distance between cities = 1,075 km
>
> cost per distance = $0.240/km
>
> **Unknown:** total cost = ?

Step 2: **Write down the equation that converts distance to cost of the flight.**

$$\text{total cost of flight} = \frac{\text{cost of flight}}{1 \text{ km of travel}} \times \text{distance between cities}$$

or

$$\text{total cost of fight} = \text{cost per distance} \times \text{distance between cities}$$

Step 3: Multiply the distance between cities by the conversion factor, and solve.

$$\text{total cost of flight} = \frac{\$0.240}{\text{km}} \times 1075 \text{ km}$$

$$\text{total cost of flight} = \$258$$

PRACTICE

1. You have been saving pennies in a jar, and you now have 125 pennies. You want to know the total mass of the pennies before you take them to the bank. If the average penny has a mass of 2.50 g, what is the total mass of the pennies?

   _____

2. You take the pennies to the bank and exchange them for nickels. Calculate the mass of 25 nickels if each nickel has a mass of 5.00 g. Which has a greater mass, $1.25 in pennies or $1.25 in nickels?

   _____

3. A hand of bananas is a small bunch made up of 5 bananas (each banana is called a finger). If a large bunch of bananas is made up of 10 hands, how many bananas does it contain?

_____

4. A tree bears 73 individual pieces of fruit each year. Suppose you own an orchard that contains 120 of these trees.

a. How much fruit will the orchard produce each year?

_____

b. The upkeep and care of the orchard costs you $850 a year. At what price will you have to sell each piece of fruit just to break even?

_____

5. A supermarket sells milk in containers of various sizes and charges consumers by the liter. How much does a plastic jug of milk with a volume of 3.79 L cost if the milk sells for $0.760/L?

_____

PROBLEM

An automobile's crankshaft makes about 2,400 revolutions each minute, or 2,400 rpm, when the car travels 65 mi/h. How many revolutions does the crankshaft make after 25 s?

SOLUTION

Step 1:   List the given and unknown values.

Given: rotation rate of crankshaft = 2,400 rpm

time engine = 25 s

Unknown: total number of revolutions = ?

Step 2:   Write down the conversion factor that converts the number of crankshaft revolutions per minute to the number of revolutions per second. Multiply revolutions per minute by minutes per second.

$$\text{rotation rate of crankshaft} = \frac{\text{revolutions}}{\text{minute}} \times \frac{\text{minutes}}{\text{second}}$$

| Math Skills *continued*

Step 3: **Multiply the time the engine runs by this conversion factor, and solve.**

$$\text{total number of revolutions} = \left(\frac{\text{revolutions}}{\text{minute}} \times \frac{\text{minutes}}{\text{second}} \right) \times \text{time engine runs}$$

$$\text{total number of revolutions} = \left(\frac{2{,}400 \text{ rev}}{\text{min}} \times \frac{1 \text{ min}}{60 \text{ s}} \right) \times 25 \text{ s}$$

$$= \frac{40 \text{ rev}}{1.0 \text{ s}} \times 25 \text{ s}$$

$$\text{total number of revolutions} = 1{,}000 \text{ rev}$$

PRACTICE

6. You are pouring hot chocolate into cups for yourself and some friends. Calculate the number of cups of hot chocolate that you can pour from a pitcher if the pitcher's volume is 4.3 L and the volume of each cup is 170 cm³.

_____

7. A pie can be cut into eight slices. What is the minimum number of pies you would need if you were to serve a slice of pie with each cup of hot chocolate in item 6? How many slices of pie would be left over?

_____

8. Although a story is often the same as a floor in a building, you cannot tell exactly how tall a building is by knowing the number of stories it has because the height of stories can vary. The International Financial Center, in Taipei, Taiwan, has 101 stories and reaches 448 m above street level. The building is about 12 m taller than Chicago's 110-story Sears Tower.

a. What is the height of each story in the Sears Tower?

_____

b. What is the height of each story in the International Financial Center?

_____

PROBLEM

Venus is the only planet in the solar system that takes a longer time to rotate than it does to revolve around the sun. As a result, a day is longer than a year on Venus. If a day on Venus equals 243.0 Earth days and a year on Venus equals 224.7 Earth days, how many Venus years are in a Venus day?

SOLUTION

Step 1: **List the given and unknown values.**

  Given: 1 Venus year = 224.7 Earth days

  1 Venus day = 243.0 Earth days

  Unknown: number of Venus years in a Venus day = ?

Step 2: **Write down the conversion factor that converts Venus days to Venus years.**

$$\frac{\text{Venus years}}{\text{Venus day}} = \frac{1 \text{ Venus year}/224.7 \text{ Earth days}}{1 \text{ Venus day}/243.0 \text{ Earth days}}$$

Step 3: **Multiply the number of Venus days by this conversion factor, and solve.**

$$\text{Venus years in a Venus day} = 1 \text{ Venus day} \times \frac{1 \text{ Venus year}/224.7 \text{ Earth days}}{1 \text{ Venus day}/243.0 \text{ Earth days}}$$

$$= \frac{243.0}{224.7} \text{ Venus years}$$

$$\text{Venus years in a Venus day} = 1.081 \text{ Venus years}$$

PRACTICE

9. Suppose you are making a 650 km trip in an automobile. The car is able to travel an average distance of 54 km on 1.0 gallon of gasoline. How much will the trip cost if the price of gasoline is $1.20/gal?

_____

10. A landfill for a county with a population of 65,000 people has a volume of approximately 2.0×10^6 m³. If the county produces 6.2×10^7 kg of garbage each year and the density of the garbage is assumed to be 410 kg/m³, how many years will it take the landfill to fill?

_____

11. A chandelier has sockets for 12 light bulbs. Suppose there are 75 of these chandeliers in an auditorium. If a box of light bulbs contains four bulbs, what is the minimum number of boxes needed to fill all of the sockets in all of the chandeliers?

_____

12. A method for obtaining water for desert areas involves the removal of salt from sea water. The simplest way to remove the salt is through distillation, a process in which sea water is evaporated and then condensed as salt-free water. If there are 26.84 g of sodium chloride in 1.00 kg of sea water, what mass of sodium chloride can be recovered from 7.400×10^6 kg of sea water?

_____

Math Skills *continued*

PROBLEM

A family in your neighborhood is moving to another state, and you are helping them pack their books ahead of time. They have 755 books, and the average book has a mass of 3.5 kg. If a box can hold 49 kg, how many boxes will be needed?

SOLUTION

Step 1: **List the given and unknown values.**

Given: number of books = 755 books

mass of each book = 3.5 kg/book

mass of book held by each box = 49 kg/book

Unknown: number of boxes = ? boxes

Step 2: **Write down the conversion factor that converts the mass of books in a box to the number of books in a box.** Divide the mass of books that a box can hold by the mass of one book.

$$\text{number of books held by each box} = \frac{\text{mass of books held by each box}}{\text{mass of each book}}$$

Step 3: **Divide the number of books by this conversion factor, and solve.**

$$\text{number of boxes} = \frac{\text{number of books}}{\left(\dfrac{\text{mass of books held by each box}}{\text{mass of each book}}\right)}$$

$$\text{number of boxes} = \frac{755 \text{ books}}{\left(\dfrac{49 \text{ kg/box}}{3.5 \text{ kg/book}}\right)} = \frac{755 \text{ books}}{14 \text{ books/box}}$$

$$\text{number of boxes} = 54 \text{ boxes}$$

PRACTICE

13. Motion pictures are shown at a speed of 24 frames, or individual pictures, each second. If a standard frame is 1.9 cm long, how long will the strand of film be for a movie that lasts 1 hour and 45 minutes?

_____

14. The Parthenon, in Athens, Greece, is one of the most recognized landmarks in the world. There are 46 Doric columns along the outer edge of the Parthenon. Each column has an average radius of 0.95 m and is 10.4 m tall. Assuming that the columns are cylindrical, what is the total volume of the columns? (Hint: The equation for the volume of a cylinder is $\pi r^2 h$, where r is the radius and h is the height.)

Skills Worksheet

Math Skills

Converting Amount to Mass

After you study each sample problem and solution, work out the practice problems on a separate sheet of paper. Write your answers in the spaces provided.

PROBLEM

Hydrogen (molar mass = 2.02 g/mol) is the most common element in the universe, and it is usually found in the molecular form H_2. Determine the mass in grams of 7.50 mol of molecular hydrogen.

SOLUTION

Step 1:   List the given and unknown values.

> **Given:**   amount of hydrogen = 7.50 mol H_2
>
> molar mass of hydrogen = 2.02 g/mol H_2
>
> **Unknown:**   mass of hydrogen = ? g

Step 2:   Write down the conversion factor that converts moles of molecular hydrogen to grams. The conversion factor you choose should have what you are trying to find (grams of H_2) in the numerator and what you want to cancel (moles of H_2) in the denominator.

$$\frac{2.02 \text{ g } H_2}{1 \text{ mol } H_2}$$

Step 3:   Multiply the amount of hydrogen in moles by the conversion factor you have chosen, and solve.

$$7.55 \text{ mol } H_2 \times \frac{2.02 \text{ g } H_2}{1 \text{ mol } H_2} = 15.3 \text{ g } H_2$$

PRACTICE

1. Uranium (molar mass = 283.03 g/mol) has the largest molar mass of any element naturally found on Earth.

   What is the mass of 7.50 mol of uranium?

   _____

2. Ruthenium (101.07 g/mol) is used as a catalyst and to improve titanium's resistance to corrosion. It is also one of the rarest elements in Earth's crust, making up less than one ten-millionth of the crust's total mass. Calculate the mass of 37.0 mol of ruthenium.

   _____

3. Large deposits of manganese (54.94 g/mol), a metal used to form many different types of alloys, have been found on the floors of oceans and large lakes. Suppose one of these deposits contains 383 mol of manganese. What is the mass of the manganese deposit?

_____

4. Sodium chloride (58.44 g/mol), commonly known as table salt, is the most common type of salt. What is the mass of 29.0 mol of sodium chloride?

_____

5. Oxygen gas is most often found as O^2 (molar mass = 32.00 mol). However, under certain conditions, a compound called ozone, O^3 (molar mass = 48.00 g/mol) is formed. Ozone, which is highly reactive and unstable, is formed when O^2 is exposed to ultraviolet radiation. Ozone is able to absorb other ultraviolet radiation, protecting life on Earth's surface from this harmful radiation.

   a. What is the mass of 17 mol of O^2?

_____

   b. What is the mass of 17 mol of O^3?

_____

6. After oxygen, silicon is the most common element found in Earth's crust. Both elements are found in silicon dioxide (molar mass = 60.09 g/mol), which is the main component in sand. Suppose you have 893 mol of silicon dioxide in a sample of sand. What is the mass of the silicon dioxide?

_____

7. Carbon dioxide (molar mass = 44.01 g/mol) is an inert gas that plants need for photosynthesis.

   a. Calculate the mass of 893 mol of carbon dioxide.

_____

   b. How does the mass you obtained in part (a) compare with the mass of 893 mol of silicon dioxide?

_____

8. Both marble and limestone contain the same mineral, calcite, which consists of the compound calcium carbonate (molar mass = 100.09 g/mol). What is the mass of a block of calcite if it contains 37 mol of calcium carbonate?

_____

Skills Worksheet

Math Skills

Converting Mass to Amount

After you study each sample problem and solution, work out the practice problems on a separate sheet of paper. Write your answers in the spaces provided.

PROBLEM

Lithium (molar mass = 6.94 g/mol) is so light that a 0.001 m³ (1 L) volume of it has a mass of only 534 g. What is the amount in moles represented by this mass of lithium?

SOLUTION
Step 1:   List the given and unknown values.

> **Given:**   mass of lithium = 534 g Li
>
> molar mass of lithium = 6.94 g/mol Li
>
> **Unknown:**   amounts of lithium = ? mol

Step 2:   Write down the conversion factor that converts grams to moles.
The conversion factor you choose should have what you are trying to find (moles of Li) in the numerator and what you want to cancel (grams of Li) in the denominator.

$$\frac{1 \text{ mol Li}}{6.94 \text{ g Li}}$$

Step 3:   Multiply the mass of lithium in grams by this conversion factor, and solve.

$$534 \text{ g Li} \times \frac{1 \text{ mol Li}}{6.94 \text{ g Li}} = 76.9 \text{ mol Li}$$

PRACTICE

1. The price of gold (molar mass = 196.97 g/mol) has varied so much over the last 30 years that with $100 you could buy as much as 2.6 troy ounces (81 g) of gold or as little as 0.13 troy ounces (4.0 g). Calculate the amount in moles that these two masses of gold represent.

_____

2. Aluminum (molar mass = 26.98 g/mol) is the most common metal in Earth's crust. But before the discovery in 1886 of the process that allowed it to be cheaply extracted from bauxite, aluminum was expensive to process. In 1852, a pound of aluminum cost $545; in 1887 the price was $0.30. At those prices, $100 would buy only 83.2 g of aluminum in 1852 but 1.51×10^5 g in 1887. Determine the amount in moles that these two masses of aluminum represent.

_____

3. Osmium (molar mass = 190.23 g/mol) and iridium (molar mass = 192.22 g/mol) have the highest densities of any elements. A cubic centimeter of either element has a mass of around 22.6 g. Determine the amount in moles of 22.6 g of each element.

_____

4. Tungsten (molar mass = 183.84 g/mol), whose high melting point makes it suitable for light bulb filaments and certain types of steel, is one of the heavier elements; its name even means "heavy stone" in Swedish. What is the amount in moles contained in a 500.0 g sample of tungsten?

_____

5. Carbon (molar mass = 12.01 g/mol) and lead (molar mass = 207.2 g/mol) are the lightest and heaviest members of their elemental group, respectively. Determine the amount in moles represented by 245 g of carbon and by 245 g of lead.

_____

6. Potassium chloride (molar mass = 74.55 g/mol) is a fairly common salt. Although it is fatal in high doses, potassium chloride can be safely consumed in small quantities. It is often mixed in small proportions with sodium chloride to produce "low-sodium" table salt. Determine the amount in moles in 150 g of potassium chloride.

_____

7. Sulfur dioxide (molar mass = 64.7 g/mol), which is formed when heated sulfur is oxidized, is a pollutant that irritates lung tissue and makes it more sensitive to dust and other particles inhaled from the outside air. Determine the amount in moles that would be represented by 27 kg of sulfur dioxide.

_____

8. Aluminum quickly oxidizes when it is exposed to air, so there is always a thin layer of aluminum oxide (molar mass = 101.96 g/mol) on any aluminum surface. This oxide layer protects the aluminum from further corrosion. If the aluminum oxide on several aluminum surfaces has a mass of 79 g, what amount in moles would be represented by this mass?

_____

9. Sulfuric acid (molar mass = 98.09 g/mol) is widely used as a corrosive reactant. It is also used in making fertilizer, detergents, drugs, explosives, and paints, and in the production of other chemicals. The usefulness of sulfuric acid is so great that it is the most widely produced chemical in the United States. What is the amount in moles in a sample of sulfuric acid that has a mass of 165 g?

Skills Worksheet

Math Skills

Writing Ionic Formulas

After you study each sample problem and solution, work out the practice problems on a separate sheet of paper. Write your answers in the space provided.

The following table lists most of the ionic formulas you will need for the Practice section. The charge on other positive ions will be indicated by a Roman numeral.

TABLE OF SOME COMMON IONS

Name	Formula	Name	Formula	Name	Formula
Aluminum ion	Al^{3+}	Bromide ion	Br^-	Carbonate ion	CO_3^{2-}
Ammonium ion	NH_4^+	Chloride ion	Cl^-	Cyanide ion	CN^-
Calcium ion	Ca^{2+}	Fluoride ion	F^-	Hydrogen carbonate ion	HCO_3^-
Lithium ion	Li^+	Iodide ion	I^-	Hydroxide ion	OH^-
Potassium ion	K^+	Nitride ion	N^{3-}	Nitrate ion	NO_3^-
Sodium ion	Na^+	Oxide ion	O^{2-}	Phosphate ion	PO_4^{3-}
Strontium ion	Sr^{2+}	Sulfide ion	S^{2-}	Sulfate ion	SO_4^{2-}

PROBLEM

Tungsten has the highest melting point of any element. It appears in nature in the mineral, *wolframite*, as the compound tungsten(VI) oxide. Write the ionic formula for this compound.

SOLUTION

Step 1: List the symbols for each ion.
Symbol for tungsten(VI) ion: W^{6+} (*VI* indicates a charge of $6\leqq$)
Symbol for oxide ion: O^{2-}

Step 2: Write the symbols for the ions with the cation first.
$W^{6+}O^{2-}$

Step 3: Find the least common multiple of the ions' charges.
The least common multiple of 6 and 2 is 6. To make a neutral compound, you need a total of six positive charges and six negative charges.
To get six positive charges, you need only one W^{6+} ion, because $1 \times 6+ = 6+$.
To get six negative charges, you need three O^{2-} ions, because $3 \times 2- = 6-$.

Step 4: Write the chemical formula, indicating with subscripts how many of each ion are needed to make a neutral compound.
WO_3

Math Skills *continued*

PRACTICE

1. Write the formulas for the following ionic compounds:

   a. potassium chloride _____

   b. tin(II) bromide _____

   c. calcium nitride _____

   d. sodium fluoride _____

2. Write the ionic formula for the compound lithium chloride.

   _____

3. Copper is found in a number of different ores, among them *cuprite* (copper(I) oxide), *nantokite* (copper(I) chloride), and *chalcocite* (copper(I) sulfide). Write the formulas for these three compounds.

   _____

4. Titanium is a metal commonly used in building airplanes and rockets, because it is light and is stronger than either steel or aluminum. Titanium is most commonly found in the form of the mineral rutile as titanium(IV) oxide. Write the ionic formula for this compound.

   _____

5. Mercury is obtained by heating the ore *cinnabar,* or mercury(II) sulfide. Write the ionic formula for mercury(II) sulfide.

   _____

6. Iridium is named after the Latin word for *rainbow* because the ionic salts it forms are of many different colors. An example of this is the two kinds of iodine compounds formed with iridium: one, iridium(III) iodide, is a green crystalline compound, while the other, iridium(IV) iodide, consists of black crystals. Write the ionic formula for each of these iridium compounds.

   _____

7. The mineral *molybdenite* is the main source of the element molybdenum, which is added to steel and other alloys to strengthen them. Molybdenite consists of the compound molybdenum(IV) sulfide. Write the ionic formula for this compound.

   _____

8. The human body needs small quantities of iodine in order for the thyroid gland to function normally. Potassium iodide is used in table salt as a dietary source of iodine. Write the ionic formula for potassium iodide.

   _____

9. Iron(III) bromide and iron(II) bromide, also known as ferric bromide and ferrous bromide, respectively, are both used in organic chemistry as catalysts. Write the ionic formula for each of these compounds.

_____

10. Calcium chloride is commonly used as a drying agent. Write the ionic formula for this compound.

_____

11. Tin(II) fluoride, also known as stannous fluoride, has been used in toothpaste to help prevent tooth decay. The presence of fluoride ions helps tooth enamel to resist attack by acids. Write the ionic formula for tin(II) fluoride.

_____

12. Write the ionic formula for the compound strontium bromide.

_____

PROBLEM

Write the ionic formula for the compound lithium phosphate.

SOLUTION

Step 1: **List the symbols for each ion.**
Symbol for lithium ion: Li^+ Symbol for phosphate ion: $(PO_4)^{3-}$

Step 2: **Write the symbols for the ions side by side, with the cation first.**
$Li^+(PO_4)^{3-}$

Step 3: **Find the least common multiple of the ions' charges.**
The least common multiple of 1 and 3 is 3. To make a neutral compound, you need a total of three positive charges and one negative charge.
To get three positive charges, you need three Li^+ ions, because $3 \times 1+ = 3+$.
To get three negative charges, you need one $(PO_4)^{-3}$ ion, because $1 \times 3- = 3-$

Step 4: **Write the chemical formula, using subscripts to indicate how many of each ion are needed to make a neutral compound.**
$Li_3(PO_4)$

PRACTICE

13. Many ionic compounds that contain calcium have been in use for so long that they are often identified by their mineral or common names, which were given to them before their chemical composition was determined. Write the ionic formulas for the following calcium compounds, whose common or mineral names are in parentheses:

    a. calcium oxide (quicklime) _____

    b. calcium fluoride (fluorite or fluorspar) _____

    c. calcium carbonate (calcite) _____

14. One of the features that has made gold attractive for centuries is that it does not lose its luster. This is because gold, unlike many metals, does not react with air or water. In fact, gold is not highly reactive at all. Nevertheless, there are a few gold compounds. Among the more common of these are gold(III) chloride and gold(I) cyanide. Write the ionic formulas for these two compounds.

    _____

15. The element manganese is used in the production of types of steel, serves as a catalyst, and is the primary source of color in amethyst. The two forms of ore from which manganese is extracted are *pyrolusite,* or manganese(IV) oxide, and *rhodochrosite,* or manganese(II) carbonate. Determine the ionic formulas for these two compounds.

    _____

16. Certain compounds change colors when water is incorporated into their crystal structure. One example of these compounds is cobalt(II) chloride, which is naturally lavender in color and turns a pinkish red when water is added. Another example is copper(II) sulfate, which turns from white to deep blue when water is added. Write the ionic formulas for these two compounds.

    _____

17. The word *chromium* is derived from the Greek word for color, and the element chromium is so named because of the bright colors that many of its compounds have. Listed below are several chromium compounds and, in parentheses, their colors. Write the ionic formulas for these compounds.

    a. chromium(VI) oxide (red) _____

    b. chromium(II) hydroxide (yellow-brown) _____

    c. chromium(III) oxide (green) _____

    d. chromium(III) chloride (violet) _____

Skills Worksheet

Math Skills

Balancing Chemical Equations

After you study each sample problem and solution, work out the practice problems on a separate sheet of paper. Write your answers in the spaces provided.

PROBLEM

Aluminum reacts with copper(II) chloride, $CuCl_2$, to form copper metal and aluminum chloride, $AlCl_3$. Write the balanced equation for this reaction.

SOLUTION

Step 1: Identify the reactants and products. Aluminum and copper(II) chloride are the reactants, and aluminum chloride and copper are the products.

Step 2: Write a word equation for the reaction.

$$\text{aluminum} + \text{copper(II) chloride} \rightarrow \text{aluminum chloride} + \text{copper}$$

Step 3: Write the equation using formulas for the elements and compounds in the word equation.

$$Al + CuCl_2 \rightarrow AlCl_3 + Cu$$

Step 4: Balance the equation one element at a time. The same number of each type of atom must appear on both sides. So far, there are three chlorine atoms on the right and only two on the left. To balance the number of chlorine atoms, you must multiply the amount of copper(II) chloride by 3 and multiply the amount of aluminum chloride by 2.

$$Al + 3CuCl_2 \rightarrow 2AlCl_3 + Cu$$

Atom	Reactants	Products	Balance
Al	1	2	no
Cu	3	1	no
Cl	6	6	yes

This equation gives you two aluminum atoms on the right and only one on the left. So you need to multiply the amount of aluminum by 2.

$$2Al + 3CuCl_2 \rightarrow 2AlCl_3 + Cu$$

Atom	Reactants	Products	Balance
Al	2	2	yes
Cu	3	1	no
Cl	6	6	yes

To balance the equation, multiply the amount of copper produced by 3.

$$2Al + 3CuCl_2 \rightarrow 2AlCl_3 + 3Cu$$

Atom	Reactants	Products	Balance
Al	2	2	yes
Cu	3	3	yes
Cl	6	6	yes

PRACTICE

1. Combustion in automobile engines takes place when fuel and oxygen are combined and ignited in the cylinders of the engine. However, the air that provides the oxygen for combustion also introduces nitrogen into the engine. The nitrogen reacts with oxygen at the high temperatures present in the engine, producing nitrogen oxide compounds, which are a major component of smog. In one of these reactions, nitric oxide, NO, reacts with oxygen, O_2, to form nitrogen dioxide, NO_2. Write the balanced equation for this reaction.

_____

2. During the centuries following the collapse of the western Roman Empire, marble (calcium carbonate, $CaCO_3$) was taken from the monuments of Rome and heated to form quicklime (calcium oxide, CaO), which was used to make plaster. Carbon dioxide, CO_2, was also produced in this decomposition reaction. Write the balanced equation for this reaction.

_____

3. When a match is lit, sulfur (S_8) reacts with oxygen to release energy and form sulfur dioxide, SO_2. Write the balanced equation for this reaction.

_____

4. Zinc reacts with water to produce zinc hydroxide, $Zn(OH)_2$, and molecular hydrogen gas, H_2. Write the balanced equation for this reaction.

_____

5. Barium, Ba, reacts with sulfur, S_8, to form barium sulfide, BaS. Write the balanced equation for this synthesis reaction.

_____

| Math Skills *continued*

6. Automobile airbags rely on the decomposition of the compound sodium azide (NaN_3) to produce the nitrogen gas, N_2, needed to rapidly inflate the bag. Sodium is also produced in the reaction. Write the balanced equation for this decomposition reaction.

_____

7. A useful single-displacement reaction involves thermite, which is a mixture of aluminum and iron oxide, Fe_2O_3. When the thermite reaches a high temperature, the components react to produce molten iron, aluminum oxide (Al_2O_3), and a great deal of energy. Write the balanced equation for the thermite reaction.

_____

8. Acid indigestion can occur when the stomach produces too much hydrochloric acid, HCl. An old and effective remedy for this involves drinking a solution of baking soda (sodium hydrogen carbonate, $NaHCO_3$), which reacts with the hydrochloric acid to produce sodium chloride (NaCl), water, and carbon dioxide. Write the balanced equation for this reaction.

_____

9. A problem with the remedy given in problem 8 for acid indigestion is that the carbon dioxide produced can cause discomfort. In many modern antacids, the active ingredient is magnesium hydroxide, $Mg(OH)_2$. When this compound reacts with the hydrochloric acid, a double-displacement reaction occurs that produces only water and magnesium chloride, $MgCl_2$. Write the balanced equation for this reaction.

_____

PROBLEM

Write the equation that describes the formation of glucose and oxygen, by means of photosynthesis, from carbon dioxide and water.

SOLUTION

Step 1: Identify the reactants and products. Carbon dioxide and water, the reactants, form glucose and oxygen, the products.

Step 2: Write a word equation for the reaction.

$$\text{carbon dioxide} + \text{water} \rightarrow \text{glucose} + \text{oxygen}$$

Step 3: Write the equation using formulas for the elements and compounds in the word equation. Some gaseous elements are molecules, not atoms. Oxygen in air is O_2, not O.

$$CO_2 + H_2O \rightarrow C_6H_{12}O_6 + O_2$$

Math Skills *continued*

Step 4: Balance the equation one element at a time. The same number of each type of atom must appear on both sides. So far, there are six carbon atoms on the right and only one on the left. To balance the number of carbon atoms, multiply the amount of carbon dioxide by 6.

$$6CO_2 + H_2O \rightarrow C_6H_{12}O_6 + O_2$$

Atom	Reactants	Products	Balance
C	6	6	yes
H	2	12	no
O	13	8	no

This equation gives you twelve hydrogen atoms on the right and only two on the left. So you need to multiply the amount of water by 6.

$$6CO_2 + 6H_2O \rightarrow C_6H_{12}O_6 + O_2$$

Atom	Reactants	Products	Balance
C	6	6	yes
H	12	12	yes
O	18	8	no

To balance the equation, multiply the amount of oxygen produced by 6.

$$6CO_2 + 6H_2O \rightarrow C_6H_{12}O_6 + 6O_2$$

Atom	Reactants	Products	Balance
C	6	6	yes
H	12	12	yes
O	18	18	yes

PRACTICE

10. Uranium reacts with fluorine gas, F_2, to form uranium(VI) fluoride, UF_6. Write the balanced equation for this synthesis reaction.

_____

11. Iron reacts with chlorine gas, Cl_2, to form iron(III) chloride, $FeCl_3$. Write the balanced equation for this synthesis reaction.

_____

12. Aluminum sulfate, $Al_2(SO_4)_3$, decomposes to form aluminum oxide, Al_2O_3, and sulfur trioxide, SO_3. Write the balanced equation for this reaction.

_____

13. Water is decomposed by electrolysis to form the gaseous products hydrogen, H_2, and oxygen, O_2. Write the balanced equation for this reaction.

_____

14. Potassium chlorate, $KClO_3$, decomposes to form potassium chloride, KCl, and oxygen gas. Write the balanced equation for this decomposition reaction.

_____

15. Chlorine gas, Cl_2, reacts with potassium bromide, KBr, to form potassium chloride and bromine, Br_2. Write the balanced equation for this single-displacement reaction.

_____

16. Aluminum reacts with lead nitrate, $Pb(NO_3)_2$, to form lead and aluminum nitrate, $Al(NO_3)_3$. Write the balanced equation for this single-displacement reaction.

_____

17. Ammonium chloride, NH_4Cl, reacts with calcium hydroxide, $Ca(OH)_2$, to form calcium chloride, $CaCl_2$, ammonia, NH, and water. Write the balanced equation for this reaction.

_____

18. Zinc reacts with hydrochloric acid, HCl, to form zinc chloride, $ZnCl_2$, and hydrogen gas. Write the balanced equation for this reaction.

_____

19. Fluorine reacts with sodium chloride, $NaCl$, to form sodium fluoride, NaF, and chlorine. Write the balanced equation for this single-displacement reaction. (**Hint:** Remember that both fluorine and chlorine have two atoms per molecule when they are in elemental form.)

_____

20. Calcium oxide, CaO, reacts with sulfur dioxide to form calcium sulfite, $CaSO_3$. Write the balanced equation for this synthesis reaction.

_____

21. In air, calcium sulfite, $CaSO$, reacts slowly with oxygen to form calcium sulfate, $CaSO_4$. Write the balanced equation for this reaction.

_____

22. When heated, mercury(II) oxide, HgO, decomposes to form mercury and oxygen. Through this reaction, Joseph Priestley demonstrated the existence of oxygen in 1774. Write the balanced equation for the decomposition of mercury(II) oxide.

_____

MIXED PRACTICE

23. Potassium nitrate, KNO_3, decomposes to form potassium nitrite, KNO_2, and oxygen gas, O_2. Write the balanced equation for this decomposition reaction.

_____

24. Antimony(V) chloride, $SbCl_5$, reacts with potassium iodide, KI, to form the products potassium chloride, KCl, iodine, I_2, and antimony(III) chloride, $SbCl_3$. Write the balanced equation for this reaction.

_____

25. Nitric acid, HNO_3, reacts with hydrogen sulfide, HS, to form nitrogen dioxide, NO_2, water, and sulfur, S. Write the balanced equation for this reaction.

_____

26. Chromium(III) oxide, Cr_2O_3, reacts with silicon to form chromium metal and silicon dioxide, SiO_2. Write the balanced equation for this reaction.

_____

27. Ammonium dichromate, $(NH_4)_2Cr_2O_7$, decomposes to form chromium(III) oxide, Cr_2O_3, nitrogen gas, N_2, and water. Write the balanced equation for this decomposition reaction.

_____

28. Iron(II) chloride, $FeCl_2$, reacts with water at high temperatures to form triiron tetraoxide, Fe_3O_4, hydrochloric acid, and hydrogen gas. Write the balanced equation for this reaction.

_____

29. Aluminum sulfate, $Al_2(SO_4)_3$, reacts with calcium hydroxide, $Ca(OH)_2$, to form aluminum hydroxide, $Al(OH)_3$, and calcium sulfate, $CaSO_4$. Write the balanced equation for this double-displacement reaction.

_____

30. Lead chloride, $PbCl_2$, reacts with sodium chromate, Na_2CrO_4, to form lead chromate, $PbCrO_4$, and sodium chloride, NaCl. Write the balanced equation for this double-displacement reaction.

_____

31. Vanadium pentoxide, V_2O_5, reacts with calcium to form vanadium metal and calcium oxide, CaO. Write the balanced equation for this reaction.

_____

Skills Worksheet

Math Skills

Molarity

After you study each sample problem and solution, work out the practice problems on a separate sheet of paper. Write your answers in the spaces provided.

PROBLEM

What is the molarity of a potassium chloride (KCl) solution that has 55.2 g of KCl dissolved in enough solvent so the total volume of the solution is 558 mL? The molar mass of KCl is 74.6 g/mol.

SOLUTION

Step 1: **List the given and unknown values.**

Given: mass of KCl = 55.2 g

volume of solution = 558 mL

molar mass KCl = 74.6 g/mol

Unknown: molarity, moles of KCl in solution

Step 2: **Write the equations for moles of KCl and molarity.**

$$moles\ KCl = \frac{mass\ KCl}{molar\ mass\ KCl}$$

$$molarity = \frac{moles\ KCl}{volume\ of\ solution\ in\ L}$$

Step 3: **Use the given values to find the number of moles of solute in the solution.**

$$moles\ KCl = \frac{55.2\ g}{74.6\ g/mol} = 0.740\ mol\ KCl$$

Step 4: **Use the newly derived value to find the molarity.**

$$molarity = \frac{0.740\ mol\ KCl}{.0558\ L} = 1.33\ M$$

PRACTICE

1. What is the molarity of a 0.75 L solution that contains 9.1 g NaCl (sodium chloride)? NaCl has a molar mass of 58 g/mol.

_____

2. A 4.25 L solution contains 181 g of sodium hypochlorite bleach, or NaOCl. NaOCl has a molar mass of 74.5 g/mol. What is the molarity of the solution?

_____

Math Skills *continued*

3. What is the molarity of a solution that contains 1.22 mol of hydrogen chloride if the total volume of the solution is 1,251 mL?

_____

4. A potassium iodide (KI) solution is known to contain 6.25 g of KI as the solute. If the total solution is 0.166 L in volume, what is its molarity? The molar mass of KI is 166 g/mol.

_____

PROBLEM

A student knows that an HCl solution has a molarity of 0.578 M and contains 3.87 g of HCl. Given that HCl has a molar mass of 36.5 g/mol, what is the volume of the solution?

SOLUTION

Step 1:   List the given and unknown values.

   Given: mass of HCl = 3.87 g

   molarity = 0.578 M

   molar mass HCl = 36.5 g/mol

   Unknown: volume of solution, moles of HCl in solution

Step 2:   Write the equations for moles of HCl and molarity. Rearrange the molarity equation to isolate volume.

$$moles\ HCl = \frac{mass\ HCl}{molar\ mass\ HCl}$$

$$molarity = \frac{moles\ HCl}{volume\ of\ solution\ in\ L}$$

$$volume\ of\ solution\ in\ L = \frac{moles\ HCl}{molarity}$$

Step 3:   Use the given values to find the number of moles of solute in the solution.

$$moles\ HCl = \frac{3.87\ g}{36.5\ g/mol} = 0.106\ mol\ HCl$$

Step 4:   Use the newly derived value to find the volume.

$$volume\ of\ solution\ in\ L = \frac{0.106\ mol}{0.578\ M} = \frac{0.106\ mol}{0.578\ mol/L} = 0.183\ L$$

Math Skills *continued*

PRACTICE

5. A solution contains 56.7 g of solute. If the solution has a molarity of 2.25 M, and the solute has a molar mass of 25.2 g/mol, what is the volume of the solute?

_____

6. An H_2SO_4 solution contains 159 g of H_2SO_4. The solution has a molarity of 0.645. If the molar mass of H_2SO_4 is given as 98.1 g/mol, what is the volume of the solution?

_____

7. How many liters of a 3.5 M NaCl solution are needed to provide 55 g of NaCl? Use 58 g/mol as the molar mass for NaCl.

_____

8. How many liters of a 0.414 M $CuSO_4$ solution are needed to provide 155 g of $CuSO_4$, given that $CuSO_4$ has a molar mass of 160 g/mol?

_____

9. If a given solution contains 3.55 mol of calcium hydroxide, and the solution has a molarity of 0.667 M, what is the volume of the solution?

_____

PROBLEM

A citric acid ($C_6H_8O_7$) solution has a molarity of 1.33 M and a volume of 2.69 L. If the molar mass of $C_6H_8O_7$ is given as 192 g/mol, what is the mass of the $C_6H_8O_7$ in the given solution?

SOLUTION

Step 1: List the given and unknown values.

       Given: volume of solution = 2.69 L

                molarity = 1.33 M

                molar mass $C_6H_8O_7$ = 192 g/mol

   Unknown: mass of $C_6H_8O_7$ in solution, moles of $C_6H_8O_7$ in solution

Step 2: Write the equations for molarity and moles of $C_6H_8O_7$. Rearrange the molarity equation to isolate moles, and rearrange the other equation to isolate the mass of the solute.

$$molarity = \frac{moles\ C_6H_8O_7}{volume\ of\ solution\ in\ L}$$

$$moles\ C_6H_8O_7 = (molarity)(volume\ of\ solution\ in\ L)$$

$$moles\ C^6H^8O^7 = \frac{mass\ C^6H^8O^7}{molar\ mass\ C^6H^8O^7}$$

$$mass\ C_6H_8O_7 = (molar\ mass\ C_6H_8O_7)(moles\ C_6H_8O_7)$$

Step 3: Use the given values to find the number of moles of solute in the solution.

$$moles\ C_6H_8O_7 = (1.33\ M)(2.69\ L) = (1.33\ mol/L)(2.69\ L)$$

$$moles\ C_6H_8O_7 = 3.58\ mol$$

Step 4: Use the newly derived value to find the mass of the solute.

$$mass\ C_6H_8O_7 = (192\ g/mol)(3.58\ mol)$$

$$mass\ C_6H_8O_7 = 687\ g$$

PRACTICE

10. What is the mass of solute that has a molar mass of 101 g/mol in a solution whose volume is 0.766 L, and whose molarity is 0.881 M?

_____

11. How many grams of glucose, $C_6H_{12}O_6$, can be found in 4.77 L of solution with a molarity of 1.11? Glucose has a molar mass of 180 g/mol.

_____

12. A science student plans to prepare a 1.25 M NaCl solution. She needs 3.25 L of solution. How many grams of NaCl will she need to create the solution? Use 58.5 g/mol for the molar mass of NaCl.

_____

13. A student wants to create a 3.11 M potassium nitrate solution. If the solution is to have a total volume of 6.25 L, how many moles of potassium nitrate does he need?

_____

_____

MIXED PRACTICE

14. How many grams of sucrose, $C_{12}H_{22}O_{11}$, would you need to make 5.25 L of a 1.11 M solution? Sucrose has a molar mass of 342 g/mol.

_____

15. What is the molarity of a lithium chloride (LiCl) solution with a volume of 2.11 L, if there are 25.1 g of LiCl in the solution? The molar mass of LiCl is 42.4 g/mol.

_____

16. You add 1,222 g of a solute to a container, and then add enough water so that the total amount of the solution is 1.220 L. If the solute has a molar mass of 115.2 g/mol, what is the molarity of the solution?

_____

17. A student wants to make 5.00 L of 1.00 M calcium chloride ($CaCl_2$) solution. If the molar mass of $CaCl_2$ is 110 g/mol, how many grams of $CaCl_2$ will she need?

_____

18. A 0.8111 M KNO_3 solution contains 2.01 g of KNO_3. If KNO_3 has a molar mass of 101.1 g/mol, how many liters of solution are present?

_____

19. A student creates a solution with a molarity of 1.55 M. If the solute has a molar mass of 110 g/mol and the solution contains 188 g of solute, what is the volume of the solution?

_____

Skills Worksheet

Math Skills

Determining pH

After you study each sample problem and solution, work out the practice problems on a separate sheet of paper. Write your answers in the spaces provided.

PROBLEM

What is the pH of a 0.001 M solution of the strong acid HI dissolved in water?

SOLUTION

Step 1: **List the given and unknown values.**

> **Given:** concentration of HI in solution ∇ 0.001 M

> **Unknown:** pH

Step 2: **Determine the molar concentration of hydroxide ions.**

concentration of HI in solution ∇ 0.001 M

HI is a strong acid, so the concentration of hydroxide ions in the solution is equal to the concentration of HI

concentration of H_3O^+ ions ∇ concentration HI = 0.001 M = 1×10^{-3} M

Step 3: **Convert the H_3O^+ concentration to pH**

pH = the negative of the power of ten used to describe the concentration of H_3O^+ ions

concentration of H_3O^+ ions = 1×10^{-3} M

pH = –(–3) = 3

PRACTICE

1. A strong acid, HBr, has been dissolved into a beaker of water. If the solution is known to be 0.000 001 M, what is the pH of the solution?

_____

2. Tetrafluoroboric acid, HBF_4, is dissolved into a 1×10^{-2} M solution. Since tetrafluoroboric acid is a strong acid, what is the pH of the solution?

_____

3. What is the pH of a 0.001 M solution of HI, a strong acid, dissolved in solution?

_____

| Math Skills *continued*

4. What is the pH of a 0.000 001 M solution of HCl, a strong acid?

_____

5. Periodic acid, HIO_4, is a strong acid. If periodic acid is dissolved in a 1×10^{-5} M solution, what is the pH of the solution?

_____

6. A given solution has HNO_3, nitric acid, dissolved in it. If the solution is a 0.001 M solution, what is its pH?

_____

7. What is the pH of a 0.000 01 M solution of the strong acid, hydrobromic acid?

_____

8. Perchloric acid, or $HClO_4$, is dissolved in a 1×10^{-2} M solution. What is the pH of the solution?

_____

PROBLEM

A solution with a pH of 4 consists of the strong acid sulfuric acid, or H_2SO_4, dissolved in water. What is the molarity of the solution?

Step 1: **List the given and unknown values.**

      Given: pH of solution = 4

      Unknown: molarity

Step 2: **Convert the pH to H_3O^+ concentration.**

      pH = the negative of the power of ten used to describe the concentration of hydronium ions

      concentration of $H_3O^+ = 1 \times 10^{-(pH)}$ M

      pH = 4

      concentration of $H_3O^+ = 1 \times 10^{-4}$ M

Step 3: **Convert the H_3O^+ concentration to acid concentration.**

      Since H_2SO_4 is a strong acid, H_3O^+ concentration = H_2SO_4 concentration

      H_3O^+ concentration = 1×10^{-4} M

      H_2SO_4 concentration = 1×10^{-4} M = 0.0001 M

PRACTICE

9. Chloric acid, $HClO_3$, is a strong acid. What is the concentration of a chloric acid solution with a pH of 2?

_____

10. What is the concentration of a hydrochloric acid (HCl) solution with a pH of 5? Hydrochloric acid is a strong acid.

_____

11. A solution is composed of the strong acid nitric acid, HNO_3, dissolved in water. If the solution has a pH of 3, what is the concentration of the solution?

_____

12. A permanganic acid ($HMnO_4$) solution has a pH of 5. Given that permanganic acid is a strong acid, what is the concentration of the solution?

_____

13. Hydrobromic acid is a strong acid. A hydrobromic acid solution has a pH of 3. What is the concentration of hydrobromic acid in the solution?

_____

14. What is the concentration of an HBF_4 solution that has a pH of 6? HBF_4 is a strong acid.

_____

15. HIO_4, or periodic acid, is a strong acid. What is the concentration of periodic acid in a solution whose pH is 1?

_____

MIXED PRACTICE

16. What is the pH of a 1×10^{-4} solution that contains dissolved $HClO_3$, a strong acid?

_____

17. What is the concentration of a solution with a pH of 3, if it contains the strong acid HI, or hydroiodic acid?

_____

18. What is the pH of a 0.01 M permanganic acid solution? Permanganic acid is a strong acid.

_____

| Math Skills *continued*

19. Sulfuric acid is a strong acid. A sulfuric acid solution has a pH of 6. What is the concentration of the solution?

_____

20. What is the concentration of a hydrochloric acid (HCl) solution with a pH of 3? Hydrochloric acid is a strong acid.

_____

21. Calculate the pH of a 1×10^{-5} solution of $HClO_3$, a strong acid.

_____

Skills Worksheet

Math Skills

Nuclear Decay

After you study each sample problem and solution, work out the practice problems on a separate piece of paper. Write your answers in the spaces provided.

PROBLEM

Polonium is the scarcest natural element and was the first to be discovered by the Curies. Write the equation for the alpha decay of polonium-210, and determine what isotope is formed by the reaction.

SOLUTION

Step 1: Write down the equation with the original element on the left side and the products on the right side.

Use the letter X to denote the unknown product. Note that the mass and atomic numbers of the unknown isotope are represented by the letters A and Z.

$$^{210}_{84}\text{Po} \rightarrow {}^{A}_{Z}X + {}^{4}_{2}\text{He}$$

Step 2: Write math equations for the atomic and mass numbers.

$$210 = A + 4 \qquad\qquad 84 = Z + 2$$

Step 3: Rearrange the equations.

$$A = 210 - 4 \qquad\qquad Z = 84 - 2$$

Step 4: Solve for the unknown values, and rewrite the equation with all nuclei represented.

$$A = 206 \qquad\qquad Z = 82$$

The unknown decay product has an atomic number of 82, which is lead, as you can see on a periodic table. The isotope is $^{206}_{82}\text{Pb}$.

$$^{210}_{84}\text{Po} \rightarrow {}^{206}_{82}\text{Pb} + {}^{4}_{2}\text{He}$$

PRACTICE

1. Radiation emitted during radon's decay process was discovered to be useful in cancer therapy. Identify the element X formed in the following reaction, in which radon-222 undergoes alpha decay.

$$^{222}_{86}\text{Rn} \rightarrow {}^{A}_{Z}X + {}^{4}_{2}\text{He}$$

2. Derived from the Greek word *astatos,* the name of the metalloid astatine means "unstable." Identify the element X formed in the reaction below, in which astatine-209 undergoes alpha decay.

$$^{209}_{85}At \rightarrow {}^{A}_{Z}X + {}^{4}_{2}He$$

3. Named after the planet Uranus, uranium is the heaviest atom among the natural elements. Identify the element X in the reaction below, in which uranium-237 undergoes alpha decay.

$$^{237}_{92}U \rightarrow {}^{A}_{Z}X + {}^{4}_{2}He$$

PROBLEM

Barium sulfate is consumed by patients undergoing certain X ray examinations. The white liquid outlines the stomach and intestines to assist doctors in making a diagnosis. Write the equation for the beta decay of barium-140, and determine what isotope is formed by the reaction.

SOLUTION

Step 1: Write down the equation with the original element on the left side and the products on the right side. Use the letter X to denote the unknown product. Note that the mass and atomic numbers of the unknown isotope are represented by the letters A and Z.

$$^{140}_{56}Ba \rightarrow {}^{A}_{Z}X + {}^{0}_{-1}e$$

Step 2: Write math equations for the atomic and mass numbers.

$$140 = A + 0 \qquad\qquad 56 = Z - 1$$

Step 3: Rearrange the equations.

$$A = 140 - 0 \qquad\qquad Z = 56 + 1$$

Step 4: Solve for the unknown values, and rewrite the equation with all nuclei represented.

$$A = 140 \qquad\qquad Z = 57$$

The unknown decay product has an atomic number of 57, which is lanthanum, according to the periodic table. The isotope is therefore $^{140}_{57}La$.

$$^{140}_{56}Ba \rightarrow {}^{140}_{57}La + {}^{0}_{-1}e$$

| Math Skills *continued*

PRACTICE

4. One cobalt radioactive isotope is used to treat cancer. Identify the element X in the reaction below, in which cobalt-60 undergoes beta decay.

$$^{60}_{27}Co \rightarrow ^{A}_{Z}X + ^{0}_{-1}e$$

5. Natural forms of carbon include diamonds, charcoal, and graphite. Identify the element X in the reaction below, in which carbon-14 undergoes beta decay.

$$^{14}_{6}C \rightarrow ^{A}_{Z}X + ^{0}_{-1}e$$

6. Discovered in 1450, bismuth is the most metallic member of its family. Identify the element X in the reaction below, in which bismuth-210 undergoes beta decay.

$$^{210}_{83}Bi \rightarrow ^{A}_{Z}X + ^{0}_{-1}e$$

PROBLEM

Lead is a highly durable element that was used in the plumbing industry for centuries. Some of the lead pipes that were used to drain the baths of ancient Rome have been uncovered still in working order. Determine whether alpha or beta decay occurs in the reaction in which lead-210 decays to bismuth-210.

SOLUTION

Step 1: Write down the equation with the original element on the left side and the products on the right side. Use the letter X to represent the unknown decay particle. The mass and atomic numbers of the unknown particle are represented by the letters A and Z.

$$^{210}_{82}Pb \rightarrow ^{210}_{83}Bi + ^{A}_{Z}X$$

Step 2: Write math equations for the atomic and mass numbers.

$$210 = 210 + A \qquad\qquad 82 = 83 + Z$$

Step 3: Rearrange the equations.

$$A = 210 - 210 \qquad\qquad Z = 82 - 83$$

| Math Skills *continued*

Step 4: Solve for the unknown values, and rewrite the equation with all nuclei represented.

$$A = 0 \qquad\qquad\qquad\qquad Z = -1$$

The unknown particle is an electron, which is emitted as a beta particle.

$$^{210}_{82}Pb \rightarrow \,^{210}_{83}Bi + \,^{0}_{-1}e$$

PRACTICE

7. Protactinium, discovered in 1917, is the third-rarest of the naturally occurring elements. Identify the decay particle emitted and the decay process that occurs when protactinium-231 decays to actinium-227.

$$^{231}_{91}Pa \rightarrow \,^{227}_{89}Ac + \,^{A}_{Z}X$$

_____

8. Samarium is one of the so-called rare earths, elements with similar chemical and physical properties that were first isolated from a mineral found in Sweden. Identify the decay particle emitted and the decay process that occurs when samarium-149 decays to form neodymium-145.

$$^{149}_{62}Sm \rightarrow \,^{145}_{60}Nd + \,^{A}_{Z}X$$

_____

9. Actinium, the second rarest of the naturally occurring elements, was discovered in 1899. Identify the emitted particle in the following reaction, and indicate whether alpha or beta decay occurs.

$$^{227}_{89}Ac \rightarrow \,^{227}_{90}Th + \,^{A}_{Z}X$$

_____

Name_____ Class _____ Date _____

Skills Worksheet

Math Skills

Half-Life

After you study each sample problem and solution, work out the practice problems on a separate piece of paper. Write your answers in the spaces provided.

PROBLEM

If 100.0 g of carbon-14 decays until only 25.0 g of carbon is left after 11,460 y, what is the half-life of carbon-14?

SOLUTION

Step 1: List the given and unknown values.

Given: initial mass of sample = 100.0g
final mass of sample = 25.0 g
total time of decay = 11,460 y

Unknown: number of half-lives = ? half-lives
half-life = ? y

Step 2: Write down the equation relating half-life, the number of half-lives, and the decay time, and rearrange it to solve for half-life.

$$\text{total time of decay} = \text{number of half-lives} \times \frac{\text{number of years}}{\text{half-life}}$$

$$\frac{\text{number of years}}{\text{half-life}} = \frac{\text{total time of decay}}{\text{number of half-lives}}$$

Step 3: Calculate how many half-lives have passed during the decay of the 100.0 g sample.

$$\text{fraction of sample remaining} = \frac{\text{final mass of sample}}{\text{initial mass of sample}} = \frac{25.0 \text{ g}}{100.0 \text{ g}} = \frac{1}{4}$$

$$\text{after one half-life} = \frac{1}{2}; \text{ after two half-lives} = \frac{1}{2} \times \frac{1}{2} = \frac{1}{4} \text{ of sample}$$

Two half-lives have passed.

Step 4: Calculate the half-life.

$$\frac{\text{number of years}}{\text{half-life}} = \frac{11,460 \text{ y}}{2 \text{ half-lives}} = \frac{5,730 \text{ y}}{\text{half-life}}$$

$$\text{half-life of carbon-14} = 5,730 \text{ y}$$

PRACTICE

1. What is the half-life of a 100.0 g sample of nitrogen-16 that decays to 12.5 g of nitrogen-16 in 21.6 s?

_____

2. All isotopes of technetium are radioactive, but they have widely varying half-lives. If an 800.0 g sample of technetium-99 decays to 100.0 g of technetium-99 in 639,000 y, what is its half-life?

_____

3. A 208 g sample of sodium-24 decays to 13.0 g of sodium-24 within 60.0 h. What is the half-life of this radioactive isotope?

_____

PROBLEM

Thallium-208 has a half-life of 3.053 min. How long will it take for 120.0 g to decay to 7.50 g?

SOLUTION

Step 1: List the given and unknown values.

Given: half-life = 3.053 min
           initial mass of sample = 120.0g
           final mass of sample = 7.50 g
Unknown: number of half-lives = ? half-lives
           total time of decay = ?

Step 2: Write down the equation relating half-life, the number of half-lives, and the decay time, and rearrange it to solve for the total time of decay.

$$\text{total time of decay} = \text{number of half-lives} \times \frac{\text{number of min}}{\text{half-life}}$$

Step 3: Calculate how many half-lives have passed during the decay of the 120.0 g sample.

$$\text{Fraction of sample remaining} = \frac{7.50\ g}{120.0\ g} = 0.0625 = \frac{1}{16}$$

$$\text{after one half-life} = \frac{1}{2};\ \text{after two half-lives} = \frac{1}{2} \times \frac{1}{2} = \frac{1}{4};$$

$$\text{after three half-lives} = \frac{1}{2} \times \frac{1}{2} \times \frac{1}{2} = \frac{1}{8};\ \text{after four half-lives} =$$

$$\frac{1}{2} \times \frac{1}{2} \times \frac{1}{2} \times \frac{1}{2} = \frac{1}{16}\ \text{of sample. Four half-lives have passed.}$$

Step 4: Calculate the total time required for the radioactive decay.

$$\text{total time of decay} = 4 \text{ half-lives} \times \frac{3.053 \text{ min}}{\text{half-life}}$$

$$\text{total time of decay} = 12.21 \text{ min}$$

PRACTICE

4. If the half-life of iodine-131 is 8.10 days, how long will it take a 50.00 g sample to decay to 6.25 g?

_____

5. The half-life of hafnium-156 is 0.025 s. How long will it take a 560 g sample to decay to one-fourth its original mass?

_____

6. Chromium-48 has a short half-life of 21.6 h. How long will it take 360.00 g of chromium-48 to decay to 11.25 g?

_____

PROBLEM

Gold-198 has a half-life of 2.7 days. How much of a 96 g sample of gold-198 will be left after 8.1 days?

SOLUTION

Step 1:   List the given and unknown values.

Given: half-life = 2.7 days
total time of decay = 8.1 days
initial mass of sample = 96 g

Unknown: number of half-lives = ? half-lives
final mass of sample = ? g

Step 2:   Write down the equation relating half-life, the number of half-lives, and the decay time, and rearrange it to solve for the number of half-lives.

$$\text{total time of decay} = \text{number of half-lives} \times \frac{\text{number of days}}{\text{half-life}}$$

$$\text{number of half-lives} = \frac{\text{total time of decay}}{\dfrac{\text{number of days}}{\text{half-life}}}$$

| Math Skills *continued*

Step 3: **Calculate how many half-lives have passed during the decay of the 96 g sample.**

$$\text{number of half-lives} = \frac{8.1 \text{ days}}{\underbrace{2.7 \text{ days}}_{\text{half-life}}} = 3.0 \text{ half-lives}$$

Step 4: Calculate how much of the sample will remain after 3.0 half-lives.

Final mass of sample = initial mass of sample × fraction of sample remaining

fraction of sample remaining after three half-lives $= \frac{1}{2} \times \frac{1}{2} \times \frac{1}{2} = \frac{1}{8}$

final mass of sample $= 96 \text{ g} \times \frac{1}{8} = 12 \text{ g}$

PRACTICE

7. Potassium-42 has a half-life of 12.4 hours. How much of an 848 g sample of potassium-42 will be left after 62.0 hours?

_____

8. Carbon-14 has a half-life of 5,730 y. How much of a 144 g sample of carbon-14 will remain after 1.719×10^4y?

_____

9. If the half-life of uranium-235 is 7.04×10^8y and 12.5 g of uranium-235 remain after 2.82×10^9y, how much of the radioactive isotope was in the original sample?

_____

Skills Worksheet

Math Skills

Velocity

After you study each sample problem and solution, work out the practice problems on a separate sheet of paper. Write your answers in the spaces provided.

PROBLEM

Polar bears are extremely good swimmers and can travel as long as 10 hours without resting. If a polar bear is swimming at an average speed of 2.6 m/s, how far will it have traveled after 10.0 hours?

SOLUTION

Step 1: **List the given and the unknown values.**

      Given: speed, $v = 2.6$ m/s

                time, $t = 10.0$ h $\times$ 3,600 s/h $= 3.6 \times 10^4$ s

      Unknown: distance, $d = ?$ m

Step 2: **Rearrange the speed equation to solve for distance.**

$$speed = \frac{distance}{time}$$

$$v = \frac{d}{t}$$

$$d = vt$$

Step 3: **Insert the known values into the equation, and solve.**

$$d = \frac{2.6 \text{ m}}{\text{s}} \times (3.6 \times 10^4 \text{ s})$$

$$d = 9.4 \times 10^4 \text{ m} = 94 \text{ km}$$

PRACTICE

1. Suppose the polar bear was running on land instead of swimming. If the polar bear runs at a speed of about 8.3 m/s, how far will it travel in 10.0 hours?

_____

2. Like the polar bear, the walrus is a strong swimmer, although it does not have the same endurance. For short periods of time, a walrus can swim at an average speed of 9.7 m/s. How far would a walrus swim at this speed in 3.4 minutes?

_____

3. The maximum posted speed limit on the U.S. Interstate Highway System is found in rural areas of several western states. This maximum speed is 75 m or 121 km/h. What is the distance, in kilometers, that a car a travels if it mo continuously at this speed for 3 hours and 20 minutes?

_____

4. For normal situations, the minimum speed limit throughout the U.S. Interstate Highway System is 45 mi/h, or 72 km/h. How far, in kilometers, will a car travel if it moves continuously at this speed for 3 hours and 20 minutes?

_____

PROBLEM

A baseball is pitched at a speed of 35.0 m/s. How long does it take the ball to travel 18.4 m from the pitcher's mound to home plate?

SOLUTION

Step 1: **List the given and the unknown values.**

Given: speed, $v = 35.0$ m/s

distance, $d = 18.4$ m

Unknown: time, $t = ?$ s

Step 2: **Rearrange the speed equation to solve for time.**

$$speed = \frac{distance}{time} \qquad v = \frac{d}{t}$$

$$tv = d \qquad \frac{t\cancel{v}}{\cancel{v}} = \frac{d}{v}$$

Step 3: **Insert the known values into the equation, and solve.**

$$t = \frac{18.4 \text{ m}}{35.0 \text{ m/s}}$$

$$t = 0.526 \text{ s}$$

PRACTICE

5. Various types of tree sloths share the honor of being the slowest-moving mammals. An average tree sloth moves at a speed of 0.743 m/s. How long does it take a sloth moving at this speed to travel 22.30 m?

_____

6. The longest stretch of straight railroad tracks lies across the desolate Nullarbor Plain, between the Australian cities of Adelaide and Perth. The tracks extend a distance of 478 km without a curve. How long would it take a train, moving at a constant speed of 97 km/h, to travel this length of track?

_____

Math Skills *continued*

7. The Concorde is the fastest supersonic passenger jet. How long would the Concorde take to travel 6,265 km between New York City and London, assuming that the jet travels at its maximum speed of 2.150×10^3 km/h during the entire trip?

_____

8. The longest distance in a track-and-field event is the 10 km run. The record holder for the women's 10 km run is Wang Junxia of China. Assuming that she ran 10.00 km at an average speed of 5.644 m/s, what was her time?

_____

PROBLEM

Florence Griffith-Joyner set the women's world record for running the 200.0 m race in 1988. At the 1988 Summer Olympics in Seoul, South Korea, she completed the distance in 21.34 s. What was Griffith-Joyner's average speed?

SOLUTION

Step 1: **List the given and the unknown values.**

Given: distance, $d = 200.0$ m

time, $t = 21.34$ s

Unknown: speed, $v = ?$ m/s

Step 2: **Write out the equation for speed.**

$$speed = \frac{distance}{time} \qquad v = \frac{d}{t}$$

Step 3: **Insert the known values into the speed equation, and solve.**

$$v = \frac{d}{t} = \frac{200.0 \text{ m}}{21.34 \text{ s}}$$

$$v = 9.372 \text{ m/s}$$

PRACTICE

9. The cheetah, the fastest of land animals, can run 274 m in 8.65 s at its top speed. What is the cheetah's top speed?

_____

10. In 1985, Matt Biondi set a record for the men's 100 m freestyle event in swimming. He took 49.17 s to swim the 50.0-m length of the pool and swim back. Assume that half of Biondi's record time was spent traveling the length of the pool. What was his speed?

_____

Name_____ Class _____ Date _____

| Math Skills *continued*

11. The fastest crossing of the Atlantic Ocean by an ocean liner was made on July 7, 1952. The ship, the SS *United States,* traveled 4,727 km east by northeast in 3 days, 10 hours, and 40 minutes. Assume that the ship had traveled the same speed, but directly east. What would the velocity of the SS *United States* be in kilometers per hour?

_____

12. The bird that migrates the farthest is the Arctic tern. Each year, the Arctic tern travels 32,000 km between the Arctic Ocean and the continent of Antarctica. Most of the migration takes place within two four-month periods each year. Assume that an Arctic tern completes the second half of its annual migration distance in 122 days. Also assume that during this time the tern flies directly north. If the tern flies the same distance each day, what is its velocity in kilometers per day?

_____

MIXED PRACTICE

13. The typical snail doesn't cover very much ground even when it is moving at its maximum speed, which is 5.0×10^{-2} m/h. How far will a snail travel if it moves at its top speed for 45 minutes?

_____

14. Motion pictures typically are filmed and shown at a speed of 24 frames per second, where a frame is a single photographic image in the film. A motion-picture camera that moves the film at 2.4×10^5 frames per second is used in high-speed photography. When the film is shown again at 24 frames per second, the filmed object seems to move very slowly. This technique is used to analyze the motion of objects, like bullets, that move too quickly to be observed by the human eye. If a frame of 16-mm film is 0.75 cm in length, how fast does the film move through the high-speed camera when the film is being exposed?

_____

15. In 1926, Gertrude Ederle was the first American woman to swim across the English Channel. At that time, she set the world record for crossing the channel with an average speed of 0.725 m/s. Assuming that the distance Ederle swam was 37.9 km (the shortest distance between England and France), how long did it take her to swim the channel?

_____

16. Bonnie Blair set the world record for women's speed skating in 1995 with an average speed of 12.9 m/s. How far would Blair have traveled at this speed in 5.00 minutes?

_____

17. Although they seem to remain unchanged, many mountains undergo steady growth. If erosion and weathering are ignored, some mountains, like the San Gabriels in southern California, grow as much as 1.0 cm in a year. If a year is considered to be exactly 365 days, what is the speed at which the San Gabriel Mountains grow in kilometers per hour?

_____

18. The Trans-Siberian Railroad is the longest single railroad in the world. Starting in Moscow, the tracks stretch 9,354 km across the Siberian frontier to Vladivostok, located at the edge of the Pacific Ocean. If you were to leave Moscow and travel on the railroad at an average speed of 90.0 km/h, how long would it take for you to reach Vladivostok?

_____

19. The largest sheep and cattle ranches in the world are in Australia. Because some of these ranches are as large in area as Connecticut, the fences needed to protect the livestock from dingos and other predators are extensive. The world's longest "dingo-proof" fence is 5,530 km long. Suppose you were to travel around this fence in a car at an average speed of 45 km/h. How long would it take you to return to your starting point?

_____

20. Stars do not appear to move because they are so far away. In truth, stars actually move at fairly high speeds. Consider the relatively close star Sirius, which is moving away from our solar system at a speed of about 17.8 km/s. How far will this star travel in 2,590 years, the time it takes for Sirius to move 1° across the sky?

_____

Skills Worksheet

Math Skills

Acceleration

After you study each sample problem and solution, work out the practice problems on a separate sheet of paper. Write your answers in the spaces provided.

PROBLEM

In 1970, Don "Big Daddy" Garlits set what was then the world record for drag racing. He started at rest and accelerated at 16.5 m/s^2 (about 1.68 times the free-fall acceleration) for 6.5 s. What was Garlits's final speed?

SOLUTION

Step 1:   List the given and unknown values.

Given: acceleration, $a = 16.5$ m/s^2

time, $t = 6.5$ s

initial speed, $initial\ v = 0$ m/s

Unknown: final speed, $final\ v = ?$ m/s

Step 2:   Rearrange the acceleration equation to solve for final speed.

$$acceleration = \frac{change\ in\ speed}{time} \qquad a = \frac{\Delta v}{t} = \frac{final\ v - initial\ v}{t}$$

$$at = \left(\frac{final\ v - initial\ v}{\cancel{t}}\right)\cancel{t}$$

$$at = final\ v - initial\ v$$

$$final\ v = at + initial\ v$$

Step 3:   Insert the known values into the acceleration equation, and solve.

$$final\ v = (16.5\ m/s^2 \times 6.5\ s) + 0\ m/s$$

$$final\ v = 110\ m/s$$

PRACTICE

1. A bicyclist accelerates at 0.89 m/s^2 during a 5.0 s interval. What is the change in the speed of the bicyclist and the bicycle?

_____

| Math Skills *continued*

2. A freight train, traveling at a speed of 18.0 m/s, begins braking as it approaches a train yard. The train's acceleration while braking is –0.33 m/s². What is the train's speed after 23 s?

_____

3. An automobile accelerates 1.77 m/s² over 6.00 s to reach the freeway speed at the end of an entrance ramp. If the car's final speed is 88.0 km/h, what was its initial speed when it began accelerating? Express your answer in kilometers per hour.

_____

_____

PROBLEM

A child sleds down a steep, snow-covered hill with an acceleration of 2.82 m/s². If her initial speed is 0.0 m/s and her final speed is 15.5 m/s, how long does it take her to travel from the top of the hill to the bottom?

SOLUTION

Step 1: List the given and unknown values.

   Given: acceleration, $a = 2.82$ m/s²

   initial speed, *initial v* $= 0.0$ m/s

   final speed, *final v* $= 15.5$ m/s

   Unknown: time, $t = ?$ s

Step 2: Rearrange the acceleration equation to solve for time.

$$acceleration = \frac{change\ in\ speed}{time} \qquad a = \frac{\Delta v}{t} = \frac{final\ v - initial\ v}{t}$$

$$\cancel{a}\left(\frac{t}{\cancel{a}}\right) = \left(\frac{final\ v - initial\ v}{t}\right)\left(\frac{\cancel{t}}{a}\right) = \frac{final\ v - initial\ v}{a}$$

$$t = \frac{final\ v - initial\ v}{a}$$

Step 3: Insert the known values into the equation, and solve.

$$t = \frac{15.5\ \text{m/s} - 0.0\ \text{m/s}}{2.82\ \text{m/s}^2} = \frac{15.5}{2.82}\ \text{s}$$

$$t = 5.50\ \text{s}$$

PRACTICE

4. Once the child in the sample problem reaches the bottom of the hill, she continues sliding along the flat, snow-covered ground until she comes to a stop. If her acceleration during this time is –0.392 m/s², how long does it take her to travel from the bottom of the hill to her stopping point?

_____

_____

| Math Skills *continued*

5. The "street" automobile with the greatest acceleration is the *Tempest*. It has an acceleration of 6.89 m/s². Suppose the car accelerates from rest to a final speed of 96.5 km/h. How long does it take the *Tempest* to reach this speed?

_____

6. The *Impact* was the first commercial electric car to be developed in over 60 years. During performance tests in 1994, the car reached a top speed of nearly 296 km/h. Suppose the car started at rest and then underwent a constant acceleration of 1.6 m/s² until it reached its top speed. How long did it take the *Impact* to reach its top speed?

_____

PROBLEM

An automobile manufacturer claims that its latest model can "go from 0 to 90" in 7.5 s. If the "90" refers to 90.0 km/h, calculate the automobile's acceleration.

SOLUTION

Step 1:   List the given and unknown values.

       Given: time, $t = 7.5$ s

               initial speed, *initial v* = 0.0 km/h

               final speed, *final v* = 90.0 km/h

    Unknown: acceleration, $a = ?$ m/s²

Step 2:   Perform any necessary conversions.

To find the final speed in meters per second, you must multiply the value for speed by the number of meters in a kilometer and divide by the number of seconds in an hour.

$$\textit{final } v = 90.0 \,\frac{\text{km}}{\text{h}} \times \frac{1000 \text{ m}}{1 \text{ km}} \times \frac{1 \text{ h}}{60 \text{ min}} \times \frac{1 \text{ min}}{60 \text{ s}}$$

$$\textit{final } v = 25.0 \text{ m/s}$$

Step 3:   Write out the equation for acceleration.

$$\textit{acceleration} = \frac{\textit{change in speed}}{\textit{time}} \qquad a = \frac{\Delta v}{t} = \frac{\textit{final } v - \textit{initial } v}{t}$$

Step 4:   Insert the known values into the equation, and solve.

$$a = \frac{\Delta v}{t} = \frac{\textit{final } v - \textit{initial } v}{t} = \frac{25.0 \text{ m/s} - 0.0 \text{ m/s}}{7.5 \text{ s}} = \frac{25.0 \text{ m/s}}{7.5 \text{ s}}$$

$$a = 3.3 \text{ m/s}^2$$

| Math Skills *continued*

PRACTICE

7. The gravitational force between Mars and an object near its surface is much lower than the force between an object on Earth's surface and Earth. If the speed of a hammer, when dropped, increases from 0.0 m/s to 15.0 m/s in 4.04 s, what is the acceleration due to the gravitational force on the surface of Mars?

_____

8. A fighter jet lands on the flight deck of an aircraft carrier that has a length of 300.0 m. The jet must reduce its speed from about 153 km/h to exactly 0 km/h in 2.0 s. What is the jet's acceleration?

_____

9. A runner whose initial speed is 29 km/h increases her speed to 31 km/h in order to win a race. If the runner takes 5.0 s to complete this increase in speed, what is her acceleration?

_____

MIXED PRACTICE

10. A certain roller coaster accelerates its cars 6.35 m/s^2 up the first incline. If this acceleration happens during the first 7.0 s of the ride, how much does the coaster's speed increase?

_____

11. The solid-fuel rocket boosters used to launch a space shuttle can lift the shuttle 45 km above Earth's surface. During that time, the shuttle undergoes an almost constant total acceleration of 6.25 m/s^2, so that its speed increases from rest to about 750 m/s. How long does it take for the shuttle to reach this speed?

_____

12. In 1995, Bonnie Blair set the world record for skating 500.0 m in 38.69 s. Suppose that she coasted to a stop on the ice after she crossed the finish line. If her initial speed was 13 m/s and her acceleration was –2.9 m/s^2, how long did it take her to stop?

_____

13. The elevators in the Landmark Tower, in Yokohama, Japan, are among the fastest in the world. They accelerate upward at 3.125 m/s^2 for 4.00 s to reach their final speed. If these elevators start at rest, what is their final speed?

_____

| Math Skills *continued*

14. A ship, with a mass of 5.22×10^7 kg, has engines that can accelerate to -0.357 m/s^2. Suppose the ship approaches the dock at a speed of 16.98 m/s. How much time does the ship need to stop?

_____

15. A dog runs on a waxed floor at an initial speed of 1.5 m/s. It slides to a stop with an acceleration of -0.35 m/s^2. How long does it take for the dog to stop?

_____

16. A certain type of rocket sled is used to measure the effects of sudden, extreme deceleration. The sled reaches a top speed of 320 km/h and then comes to a complete stop in 0.18 s. What is the acceleration that takes place in this time?

_____

17. The Sears Tower in Chicago is 110 stories (436 m) above street level, and the roof of the tower is 442 m above the street. Assume that a golf ball is thrown down from the roof of the Sears Tower. Neglecting air resistance, the golf ball accelerates at 9.8 m/s^2 and lands on the pavement after 9.2 s. If the ball's final speed is 93.0 m/s, what was the speed with which the ball was initially thrown?

_____

18. In the theory of *plate tectonics,* various segments of Earth's crust, called *plates,* move toward and away from each other. In one instance, the plate that consists of the Indian subcontinent drifted from southeastern Africa to its current position in Asia, traveling at a speed of 15 cm/y. This plate collided with Asia, forming the Himalayan mountain range in the process. Most of this formation occurred during the last 1.00×10^7 years, during which time the Indian subcontinent's motion has slowed to about 5 cm/y. What has been the acceleration, in units of cm/y^2, of the Indian subcontinent during this time period?

_____

Skills Worksheet

Math Skills

Newton's Second Law

After you study each sample problem and solution, work out the practice problems on a separate sheet of paper. Write your answers in the spaces provided.

PROBLEM

The force of gravity between the moon and an object near its surface is much smaller than the force of gravity between Earth and the same object near Earth's surface. A bowling ball with a mass of 7.51 kg is pulled downward with an unbalanced force of −12.2 N. What is the acceleration of the falling bowling ball on the moon?

SOLUTION

Step 1: List the given and unknown values.

> **Given:** *mass, m* = 7.51 kg
>
> *unbalanced force , F* = 12.2 N
>
> **Unknown:** *acceleration, a* = ? m/s^2

Step 2: Rearrange the equation for Newton's second law to solve for acceleration.

$$force = mass \times acceleration \qquad F = ma$$

$$\frac{F}{m} = \frac{\cancel{m}a}{\cancel{m}} = a$$

$$a = \frac{F}{m}$$

Step 3: Insert the known values into the equation, and solve.

$$a = \frac{12.2 \text{ N}}{7.51 \text{ kg}} = \frac{12.2 \text{ kg} \cdot \text{m/s}^2}{7.51 \text{ kg}}$$

$$a = 1.62 \text{ m/s}^2$$

PRACTICE

1. The gravitational force that Earth exerts on the moon equals 2.03×10^{20} N. The moon's mass equals 7.35×10^{22} kg. What is the acceleration of the moon due to Earth's gravitational pull?

_____

2. Assume that a catcher in a professional baseball game exerts a force of −65.0 N to stop the ball. If the baseball has a mass of 0.145 kg, what is its acceleration as it is being caught?

_____

3. A type of elevator called a *cage* is used to raise and lower miners in a mine shaft. Suppose the cage carries a group of miners down the shaft. If the unbalanced force on the cage is 60.0 N, and the mass of the loaded cage is 1.50×10^2 kg, what is the acceleration of the cage?

4. A 214 kg boat is sinking in the ocean. The force of gravity that draws the boat down is partially offset by the buoyant force of the water, so the net unbalanced force on the boat is –1,310 N. What is the acceleration of the boat?

PROBLEM

A freight train slows down as it approaches a train yard. If a force of -3.8×10^6 N is required to provide an acceleration of -0.33 m/s^2, what is the train's mass?

SOLUTION

Step 1: **List the given and unknown values.**

Given: *unbalanced force, $F = -3.8 \times 10^6$ N*

acceleration, $a = -0.33$ m/s^2

Unknown: *mass, $m = ?$ kg*

Step 2: **Rearrange the equation for Newton's second law to solve for mass.**

$$force = mass \times acceleration \qquad\qquad F = ma$$

$$\frac{F}{a} = \frac{m\cancel{a}}{\cancel{a}} = m$$

$$m = \frac{F}{a}$$

Step 3: **Insert the known values into the equation, and solve.**

$$m = \frac{-3.8 \times 10^6 \text{ N}}{-0.33 \text{ m/s}^2} = \frac{-3.8 \times 10^6 \text{ kg} \cdot \text{m/s}^2}{-0.33 \text{ m/s}^2}$$

$$m = 1.15 \times 10^7 \text{ kg}$$

PRACTICE

5. The tallest man-made structure at present is the *Warszawa Radio* mast in Warsaw, Poland. This radio mast rises 646 m above the ground, nearly 200 m more than the Sears Tower in Chicago. Suppose a worker at the top of the *Warszawa Radio* mast accidentally knocks a tool off the tower. If the force acting on it is 3.6 N, and its acceleration is 9.8 m/s^2, what is the tool's mass?

Name_____ Class_____ Date_____

6. The whale shark is the largest of all fish and can have the mass of three adult elephants. Suppose that a crane is lifting a whale shark into a tank for delivery to an aquarium. The crane must exert an unbalanced force of 2.5×10^4 N to lift the shark from rest. If the shark's acceleration while being lifted equals 1.25 m/s^2, what is the shark's mass?

_____

7. A house is lifted from its foundations onto a truck for relocation. The unbalanced force lifting the house is 2,850 N. This force causes the house to move from rest to an upward speed of 0.15 m/s in 5.0 s. What is the mass of the house?

_____

8. Because of a frictional force of 2.6 N, a force of 2.8 N must be applied to a textbook in order to slide it along the surface of a wooden table. The book accelerates at a rate of 0.11 m/s^2.

   a. What is the unbalanced force on the book?

_____

   b. What is the mass of the book?

_____

PROBLEM

The most massive train was put together in South Africa in 1989 and traveled 861 km. This freight train was over 7 km long and had a total mass of 6.94×10^7 kg. Suppose the train's acceleration from rest to an average speed of 38 km/h was 0.191 m/s^2. What then would be the size of the unbalanced force that the locomotives exerted on the cars of the train?

SOLUTION

Step 1: List the given and unknown values.

   Given: *mass, m* = 6.94×10^7 kg

              acceleration, a = 0.191 m/s^2

   Unknown: *unbalanced force, F* = ? N

Step 2: Write out the equation for Newton's second law.

   force = mass × acceleration

   F = ma

Step 3: Insert the known values into the equation, and solve.

   $F = (6.94 \times 10^7$ kg$) \times (0.191$ m/s$^2)$

   $F = 1.33 \times 10^7$ kg • m/s^2 = 1.33×10^7 N

Math Skills *continued*

PRACTICE

9. In drag racing, acceleration is more important than speed, and therefore drag racers are designed to provide high accelerations. Suppose a drag racer has a mass of 1,250 kg and accelerates at a constant rate of 16.5 m/s². How large is the unbalanced force acting on the racer?

_____

10. A 5.22×10^7 kg luxury cruise ship is moving at its top speed as it comes into port. The ship then undergoes acceleration equal to –0.357 m/s² until it comes to rest at its anchorage. How large must the unbalanced force acting on the ship be in order to bring the ship to rest at the proper location?

_____

11. The force that stops a jet plane as it lands on the flight deck of an aircraft carrier is provided by a series of arresting cables. These cables act like extremely stiff rubber bands, stretching enough to keep from slowing the plane down too suddenly. A Hornet jet with a mass of 1.3×10^4 kg lands with an acceleration of –27.6 m/s². How large is the unbalanced force that the arresting cables exert on the plane?

_____

12. The giant sequoia redwood trees of the Sierra Nevada Mountains in California are said never to die from old age. Instead, an old tree dies when its shallow roots become loosened and the tree falls over. Removing a dead mature redwood from a forest is no easy feat, as the tree can have a mass of nearly 2.0×10^6 kg. Suppose a redwood with this mass is lifted with an upward acceleration of 0.85 m/s². How large is the unbalanced force lifting the tree?

_____

MIXED PRACTICE

13. Until it was recently discontinued, the fastest jet plane in the skies was the Lockheed SR-71 Blackbird. However, this plane did not reach its high speeds through large acceleration. The plane had a mass of 7.7×10^4 kg and was driven by an estimated unbalanced force of about 7.23×10^5 N. What was the acceleration of the Lockheed SR-71?

_____

14. Suppose an empty grocery cart rolls downhill in a parking lot. The cart has a maximum speed of 1.3 m/s when it hits the side of the store and comes to rest 0.30 s later. If an unbalanced force of –65 N stops the cart, what is the mass of the grocery cart?

_____

| Math Skills *continued*

15. The fastest speed achieved on Earth for any object, with the exception of subatomic particles in particle accelerators, is 15.8 km/s. A device at Sandia Laboratories in Albuquerque, New Mexico, uses highly compressed air to accelerate a small metal disk to supersonic speeds. Suppose the disk reaches its top speed from rest in 1.0 s. If the disk has a mass of 0.20 g, what is the unbalanced force on the disk?

_____

16. "Maglev" trains use magnetic fields to levitate the train a few centimeters above the tracks. This design cuts down on friction so that the train can travel much faster than trains that roll on the tracks. The fastest maglev train is an experimental Shinkansen train consisting of three cars. This train has reached a speed of 550 km/h. Assume that the mass of this train is 1.33×10^5 kg and that the unbalanced force needed to accelerate the train to its top speed is 7.07×10^4 N. What is the train's acceleration?

_____

17. *Meteorites* are rocks that enter Earth's atmosphere and only partially burn up during entry, so that the remaining mass lands on Earth's surface. The speeds with which meteorites strike Earth's surface depend on their point of origin. If they were originally small rocks that orbited Earth, their impact speed might be as low as 10.0 km/s. If the small rocks orbited the sun, the speed with which they collide with Earth could be as large as 70.0 km/s. Suppose a meteorite collides with Earth with a force of -6.41×10^{12} N.

a. What is the mass of the meteorite if its impact speed is 10 km/s, so that it has an acceleration of approximately -1.00×10^8 m/s^2 ?

_____

b. What is the mass of the meteorite if its impact speed is 70 km/s, so that it has an acceleration of approximately -490×10^9 m/s^2?

_____

18. The largest acceleration that a human has ever endured occurred when a race car accidentally crashed into a wall. The car was traveling at a speed of 172.8 km/h when it hit the wall. The car came to a complete stop 2.72×10^{-2} s later.

a. Calculate the acceleration of the car using the acceleration formula. Express your answer in both m/s^2 and in "g's." One g is equal to the free-fall acceleration of 9.8 m/s^2.

_____

b. Suppose the driver of the car had a mass of 70.0 kg. What was the unbalanced force on his body as the car underwent negative acceleration?

_____

Skills Worksheet

Math Skills

Momentum

After you study each sample problem and solution, work out the practice problems on a separate sheet of paper. Write your answers in the spaces provided.

PROBLEM

Thoroughbred horses are among the fastest horses in the world and are used in famous racing events such as the Kentucky Derby. The mass of a thoroughbred is about 5.00×10^2 kg. If a horse with this mass is galloping with a momentum of 8.22×10^3 kg • m/s, what is its speed?

SOLUTION

Step 1: List the given and unknown values.

> **Given:**   *mass, m* $= 5.00 \times 10^2$ kg
>
>   *momentum, p* $= 8.22 \times 10^3$ kg • m/s
>
> **Unknown:**   *speed, v* $= ?$ m/s

Step 2: Rearrange the momentum equation to solve for speed.

> *momentum = mass × speed* $p = mv$
>
> Error! Objects cannot be created from editing field codes.
>
> Error! Objects cannot be created from editing field codes.

Step 3: Insert the known values into the equation, and solve.

$$v = \frac{8.22 \times 10^3 \text{ kg} \bullet \text{m/s}}{5.00 \times 10^2 \text{ kg}}$$

$$v = 16.4 \text{ m/s}$$

PRACTICE

1. A pitcher in a professional baseball game throws a fastball, giving the baseball a momentum of 5.83 kg • m/s. Given that the baseball has a mass of 0.145 kg, what is its speed?

_____

Math Skills *continued*

2. The maximum speed measured for a golf ball is 273 km/h. If a golf ball with a mass of 47 g had a momentum of 5.83 kg • m/s, the same as that of the baseball in the previous problem, what would its speed be? How does this speed compare to a golf ball's maximum measured speed?

3. The World Solar Challenge in 1987 was the first car race in which all the vehicles were solar powered. The winner was the *GM Sunraycer,* which had a mass of 177.4 kg, not counting the driver's mass. Assume that the driver had a mass of 61.5 kg, so that the total momentum of the car and driver was 4.416×10^3 kg • m/s. What was the car's speed in m/s and km/h?

PROBLEM

Although larger than the Atlantic walrus, the Pacific walrus can swim with a speed of about 9.7 m/s. If the momentum of a swimming walrus is 1.07×10^4 kg • m/s, what is its mass?

SOLUTION

Step 1: List the given and unknown values.

   Given: *speed, v* = 9.7 m/s

   momentum, p = 1.07×10^4 kg • m/s

   Unknown: *mass, m* = ? kg

Step 2: Rearrange the momentum equation to solve for mass.

$$momentum = mass \times speed \qquad p = mv$$

$$\frac{p}{v} = \frac{m\cancel{v}}{\cancel{v}}$$

$$m = \frac{p}{v}$$

Step 3: Insert the known values into the equation, and solve.

$$m = \frac{1.07 \times 10^4 \text{ kg} \cdot \text{m/s}}{9.7 \text{ m/s}}$$

$$m = 1.1 \times 10^3 \text{ kg}$$

PRACTICE

4. The lightest pilot-driven airplane ever built was the *Baby Bird.* Suppose the *Baby Bird* moves along the ground without a pilot at a speed of 88.0 km/h. Under these circumstances, the momentum of the empty plane would be only 2,790 kg • m/s. What is the mass of the plane?

5. The most massive automobile to have been manufactured on a regular basis was the Russian-made Zil-41047. If one of these cars was to move at just 8.9 m/s, its momentum would be 2.67×10^4 kg • m/s. Use this information to calculate the mass of a Zil-41047.

_____

6. The brightest, hottest, and biggest stars are the brilliant blue stars designated as spectral class O. As is the case of all stars, class O stars move with speeds that are measured in km/s.

a. If a class O star moves with a speed of 255 km/s and has a momentum of 8.62×10^{36} kg • m/s, what is the star's mass?

_____

b. A class O star typically has a mass of at least 10 solar masses (that is, 10 times the mass of the sun, which is 1.99×10^{30} kg). Express the mass calculated in part a in terms of solar masses.

_____

PROBLEM

The Shinkansen, Japan's high-speed "bullet train," consists of several different versions of trains. The 100-series trains consist of 16 steel cars that have a combined mass of 9.25×10^5 kg. The top speed of a regular 100-series train is 220 km/h. What would be the momentum of one of these trains?

SOLUTION

Step 1:   List the given and unknown values.

   Given: *mass, m* = 9.25 10^5 kg

   speed, v = 220 km/h

   Unknown: *momentum, p* = ?

Step 2:   Perform any necessary conversions.

To find the speed in m/s, the value for speed must be multiplied by the number of meters in a kilometer and divided by the number of seconds in an hour.

$$v = 220 \frac{km}{h} \times \frac{1000 \text{ m}}{1 \text{ km}} \times \frac{1 \text{ h}}{60 \text{ min}} \times \frac{1 \text{ min}}{60 \text{ s}}$$

$$v = 61 \text{ m/s}$$

Step 3:   Write the equation for momentum.

$$momentum = mass \times speed \qquad p = mv$$

Step 4:   Insert the known values into the equation, and solve.

$$p = (9.25 \times 10^5 \text{ kg}) \times (61 \text{ m/s})$$
$$p = 5.6 \times 10^7 \text{ kg} \cdot \text{m/s}$$

PRACTICE

7. The 300-series Shinkansen trains consist of 16 aluminum cars with a combined mass of 7.10×10^5 kg. The reduction in mass from the 100-series enables the 300-series trains to reach a top speed of 270 km/h. What is the momentum of one of these trains at its top speed? Is the momentum of a 300-series train greater or less than the momentum of a 100-series train traveling at its top speed?

_____

8. The largest animal ever to have lived on Earth is the blue whale. Consider a blue whale with a mass of 1.46×10^5 kg and a top swimming speed of 24 km/h. What is the momentum of this whale at this speed?

_____

9. In 1996, Michael Johnson ran 200.0 m in 19.32 s. Johnson's mass at the time of his record-breaking run was about 77 kg. What was his momentum at his average speed?

_____

MIXED PRACTICE

10. The highest land speed for a rail-guided vehicle was set in 1982 by a rocket sled at Holloman Air Force Base in southern New Mexico. The sled was unmanned, but if it had a payload with a mass of 25 kg, the payload's momentum would have been about 6.8×10^4 kg • m/s. What was the speed, in m/s and km/h, of the payload and sled?

_____

11. The largest species of hummingbird is the *Patagonia gigas,* or the giant hummingbird of the Andes. This bird has a length of 21 cm and can fly with a speed of up to 50.0 km/h. Suppose one of these hummingbirds flies at this top speed. If its momentum is 0.278 kg • m/s, what is the hummingbird's mass?

_____

12. Although it cannot sustain its top speed for more than 8.65 s, the cheetah can run a distance of 274 m during that time. If a cheetah with a mass of 50.0 kg is moving at top speed, what is its momentum?

_____

13. The fastest speed recorded for a race car in the Indianapolis 500 was set in 1996 during a pre-race qualifying round. The minimum mass for a race car in the United States is 705 kg, so the minimum momentum of the record-setting car would have been 7.49×10^4 kg • m/s. What was the car's speed in both m/s and km/h?

14. A hovercraft—also known as an air-cushion vehicle—glides on a cushion of air, allowing it to travel with equal ease on land or water. The first commercial hovercraft to cross the English Channel, the V. A-3, had an average speed of 96 km/h. Its momentum at this speed was 4.8×10^4 kg • m/s. What was the mass of the V. A-3?

15. The danger that space debris poses to a spacecraft can be understood in terms of momentum. At 160 km above Earth's surface, any object will have a speed of about 7.82×10^3 m/s. Consider a meteoroid (a small orbiting rock) that is about half a meter in diameter and has a mass of 423 kg. What is its momentum? How does this compare to the momentum of one car of a 100-series Shinkansen train, from the sample problem on the previous page, traveling at top speed?

16. The fastest helicopter, the Westland Lynx, has a mass of 3.343×10^3 kg and a maximum momentum of 3.723×10^5 kg • m/s. What is its top speed?

17. A student with a mass of 55 kg rides a bicycle at a speed of 5.0 m/s. The momentum of the bicycle and rider equals 320 kg • m/s.

a. What is the combined mass of the student and bicycle?

b. How fast would the bicycle alone have to move in order to have the same momentum as that of the student and bicycle together?

18. The S.S. *Norway* is a passenger ship with a mass of 6.9×10^7 kg and a top cruising speed of 33 km/h. What is the momentum of the S.S. *Norway* once it has reached its top cruising speed?

Skills Worksheet

Math Skills

Work

After you study each sample problem and solution, work out the practice problems on a separate sheet of paper. Write your answers in the spaces provided.

PROBLEM

A car has run out of gas. Fortunately, there is a gas station nearby. You must exert a force of 715 N on the car in order to move it. By the time you reach the station, you have done 2.72×10^4 J of work. How far have you pushed the car?

SOLUTION

Step 1: List the given and unknown values.

> **Given:** *force, $F = 715$ N*
>
> *work, $W = 2.72 \times 10^4$ J*
>
> **Unknown:** *distance, $d = ?$ m*

Step 2: Rearrange the work equation to solve for distance.

$$work = force \times distance \qquad W = Fd$$

$$\frac{W}{F} = \frac{\cancel{F}d}{\cancel{F}} = d$$

Step 3: Insert the known values into the equation, and solve.

$$d = \frac{2.72 \times 10^4 \text{ J}}{715 \text{ N}} = \frac{2.72 \times 10^4 \text{ N} \cdot \text{m}}{715 \text{ N}}$$

$$d = 38.0 \text{ m}$$

PRACTICE

1. You must exert a force of 4.5 N on a book to slide it across a table. If you do 2.7 J of work in the process, how far have you moved the book?

   _____

2. A catcher picks up a baseball from the ground. If the unbalanced force on the ball is 7.25×10^{-2} N and 4.35×10^{-2} J of work is done to lift the ball, how far does the catcher lift the ball?

   _____

3. The smallest bird is the Cuban bee hummingbird, which has a mass of only 1.7 g. If this bird did 8.8×10^{-4} J of work by exerting an upward force of 3.4×10^{-4} N, how far did it fly?

PROBLEM

A building under construction requires building materials to be raised to the upper floors by cranes or elevators. A quantity of cement is lifted 76.2 m by a crane, which exerts a force on the cement that is slightly larger than the weight of the cement. If the work done in excess of the work done against gravity is 1.31×10^3 J, what is the unbalanced, overall force exerted on the cement?

SOLUTION

Step 1: List the given and unknown values.

$$\text{Given:} \quad \textit{distance, } d = 76.2 \text{ m}$$
$$\textit{work, } W = 1.31 \times 10^3 \text{ J}$$
$$\text{Unknown:} \quad \textit{force, } F = ? \text{ N}$$

Step 2: Rearrange the work equation to solve for force.

$$\textit{work} = \textit{force} \times \textit{distance} \qquad W = Fd$$

$$\frac{W}{d} = \frac{F\cancel{d}}{\cancel{d}} = F$$

Step 3: Insert the known values into the equation, and solve.

$$F = \frac{1.31 \times 10^3 \text{ J}}{76.2 \text{ m}} = \frac{1.31 \times 10^3 \text{ N} \cdot \text{m}}{76.2 \text{ m}}$$

$$F = 17.2 \text{ N}$$

PRACTICE

4. The world's most powerful tugboats are built in Finland. One of these boats can do 9.8×10^7 J of work through a distance of 35 m. What is the force exerted by the tugboat?

_____

5. A child pulls a sled up a snow-covered hill. In the process, the child does 405 J of work on the sled. If she walks a distance of 15 m up the hill, how large a force does she exert on the sled?

_____

6. One of the most powerful forklifts was built in Sweden in 1991. The lift is capable of lifting a 9.0×10^4 kg mass a distance of 2.0 m above the ground. If the work done by the forklift on the mass is 1.8×10^6 J, what is the force that the lift exerts on the mass?

_____

| Math Skills *continued*

PROBLEM

An old house is being lifted by a type of crane from its foundation and moved by truck to another location. If the house, which weighs just under 1.50×10^4 N, is lifted 1.52 m from the foundation to the bed of the truck, what is the minimum amount of work done by the crane on the house?

SOLUTION

Step 1: List the given and unknown values.

Given: *force, F* = 1.50×10^4 N
        distance, d = 1.52 m

Unknown: *work, W* = ? J

Step 2: Write out the equation for work.

$$work = force \times distance \qquad W = Fd$$

Step 3: Substitute force and distance values into the work equation, and solve.

$$W = (1.50 \times 10^4 \text{ N}) \times 1.52 \text{ m} = 2.28 \times 10^4 \text{ N} \bullet \text{m}$$
$$W = 2.28 \times 10^4 \text{ J}$$

PRACTICE

7. After the house in the sample problem has been set on the truck bed, the truck accelerates until it reaches a constant speed. If the force required to move the house horizontally a distance of 75.5 m is 3,150 N, how much work has been done on the house?

_____

8. The largest passenger ship still in service is the SS *Norway,* which has a mass of 7.6×10^7 kg. The force required to accelerate the SS *Norway* from rest to its top cruising speed of 33 km/h is 1.6×10^6 N, assuming that this acceleration takes place over a distance of 2.0 km. How much work must be done on the ship during this period of acceleration?

_____

9. Suppose an adult blue whale is stranded on a beach. The whale, which lies parallel to the shore, is 15 m from water deep enough for it to swim away in. A group of people line up along the side of the whale to push it back into the ocean. If the whale's weight is 1.5×10^6 N, and the force of friction that must be overcome by the people is 0.25 times the whale's weight, how much work must the people do on the whale in order to return it to the ocean?

_____

MIXED PRACTICE

10. A mover is loading a 253 kg crate of hammers onto a truck. The upward force on the crate is 2,470 N, and 3,650 J of work are required to raise the crate from the pavement to the truck bed. How far is the crate lifted?

_____

11. The mover in problem 10 uses a ramp, which makes the task easier by requiring a smaller force to raise the crate to the truck bed. This force must be exerted over a greater distance, so the work done should be the same. In reality, because of the frictional force between the crate and the ramp, the work required is greater than that needed to lift the crate directly onto the truck. The mover does 4,365 J of work sliding the crate up the ramp. The force the mover exerts on the crate is 1,302 N. How long is the ramp?

_____

12. A popular and dangerous circus act is the human cannonball, in which a person is shot from a cannon. Suppose the cannon has a barrel that is 3.05 m long and 1.67×10^4 J of work is done to accelerate the acrobat. What is the force exerted by the cannon on the acrobat?

_____

13. The highest occupied floors of any building are in the Sears Tower in Chicago. The elevators of the central tower of the building lift passengers 436 m above street level. If a continuous force of 2.23×10^4 N is exerted on one of these elevator cars as it travels from the ground to the top floor, how much work is done on the elevator car by the elevator's lifting mechanism?

_____

14. A freight train leaving a train yard must exert a force of 2.53×10^6 N in order to increase its speed from rest to 17.0 m/s. During this process, the train must do 1.10×10^9 J of work. How far does the train travel?

_____

15. In 1947, Northrop Aircraft developed and built a deceleration sled to test the effects of extreme forces on humans and equipment. In this sled, a test pilot with a mass of 70.0 kg undergoes a sudden negative acceleration of 4.90×10^2 m/s^2. This deceleration occurs over a distance of 8.05 m. How much work is done against the pilot's body during the deceleration?

_____

Skills Worksheet

Math Skills

Power

After you study each sample problem and solution, work out the practice problems on a separate sheet of paper. Write your answers in the spaces provided.

PROBLEM

The world's most powerful tugboats, which are built in Finland, are capable of providing 8.17×10^6 W of power. How much work does one of these tugboats do in 12.0 s?

SOLUTION

Step 1: List the given and unknown values.

Given: *power, $P = 8.17 \times 10^6$ W*

time, $t = 12.0$ s

Unknown: *work, $W = ?$ J*

Step 2: Rearrange the power equation to solve for work.

$$power = \frac{work}{time} \qquad P = \frac{W}{t}$$

$$P \times t = \frac{W}{t} \times t = W$$

Step 3: Insert the known values into the equation, and solve.

$$W = (8.17 \times 10^6 \text{ W}) \times (12.0 \text{ s}) = (8.17 \times 10^6 \text{ J/s}) \times (12.0 \text{ s})$$
$$W = 9.80 \times 10^7 \text{ J}$$

PRACTICE

1. One horsepower (1 hp) is the unit of power based on the work that a horse can do in one second. This is defined, in English units, as a force of 550 lb that can move an object 1 ft in 1 s. In SI, 1 hp equals 745.7 W. Suppose you have a horse that has a power output of 750 W. How much work does this horse do in 0.55 s?

_____

2. A race car with a 255 hp (1.90×10^5 W) engine is able to accelerate from rest to its top speed in 9.00 s. How much work does the car's engine do in this interval of time?

_____

3. A ship's diesel engine has a power output of 13.0 W (13.0×10^6 W). How much work is done by this engine in 15.0 min?

PROBLEM

Suppose a weightlifter's power output is 178 W during the time he does 3,310 J of work on the weights. How long does it take the weightlifter to raise the weights?

SOLUTION

Step 1: **List the given and unknown values.**

Given: *power, P* = 178 W

work, W = 3,310 J

Unknown: *time, t* = ? s

Step 2: **Rearrange the power equation to solve for time.**

$$power = \frac{work}{time} \qquad P = \frac{W}{t}$$

$$P \times \frac{t}{P} = \frac{W}{t} \times \frac{t}{P} = \frac{W}{P}$$

Step 3: **Insert the known values into the equation, and solve.**

$$t = \frac{3310 \text{ J}}{178 \text{ W}} = \frac{3310 \text{ J}}{178 \text{ J/s}}$$

$$t = 18.6 \text{ s}$$

PRACTICE

4. In order to sail through the frozen Arctic Ocean, the most powerful icebreaker ever built was constructed in the former Soviet Union. At the heart of the ship's power plant is a nuclear reactor with a power output of 5.60×10^7 W. How long will it take for this power plant to do 5.35×10^{10} J of work?

_____

5. The heaviest loads ever raised were part of the offshore Ekofisk complex in the North Sea. The 4.0×10^7 kg complex was raised 6.5 m by over a hundred hydraulic jacks. The work done on the complex during the raising was approximately 2.6×10^{11} J. Suppose the power output of all the jacks was 5.7×10^8 W. How long did it take the jacks to raise the complex?

_____

6. Borax was mined in Death Valley, California, during the nineteenth century. It was transported from the valley by massive wagons, each pulled by a team of 21 mules. Suppose each mule's power output was 746 W (about 1 hp). If in a certain time interval the total work done by the team on the wagon was 2.35×10^7 J, how long was that interval of time?

_____

Math Skills *continued*

PROBLEM

A certain crane is able to lift 2.20×10^6 kg. If the crane is able to raise this mass a distance of 20.0 m by doing 4.32×10^8 J of work in 35.0 s, how much power has the crane provided?

SOLUTION

Step 1: **List the given and unknown values.**

Given: *work,* $W = 4.32 \times 10^8$ J

time, $t = 35.0$ s

The distance of 20.0 m and the mass of 2.20×10^6 kg are not needed to calculate power.

Unknown: *power,* $P = ?$ W

Step 2: **Write out the equation for power.**

$$power = \frac{work}{time} \qquad P = \frac{W}{t}$$

Step 3: **Insert the known values into the equation, and solve.**

$$P = \frac{4.32 \times 10^8 \text{ J}}{35 \text{ s}} = 1.2 \times 10^7 \text{ J/s} = 1.2 \times 10^7 \text{ W}$$

$$P = 12 \text{ MW}$$

PRACTICE

7. A certain steam turbine is designed to be used as both a power generator and as a pump. When used as a generator, the turbine provides enough power to do 3×10^{10} J of work in 1 min. What is the power output of the turbine?

_____

8. The space shuttle, which was first launched on April 12, 1981, is the world's first reusable space vehicle. The shuttle is placed in orbit by three engines that do 1.4×10^{13} J of work in 8.5 min. What is the power output of these engines?

_____

9. Lithuania's major nuclear power plant has one of the world's most powerful generators, which has a power output of 1.45×10^9 W. How long must this generator run if it is to provide the energy to do 4.35×10^{11} J of work?

_____

Skills Worksheet

Math Skills

Mechanical Advantage

After you study each sample problem and solution, work out the practice problems on a separate sheet of paper. Write your answers in the spaces provided.

PROBLEM

A wheelbarrow has a mechanical advantage of 2.2. The output distance extends from the load's center of mass to the wheel, and the input distance is from the handles to the wheel. For an output distance of 0.45 m, what is the input distance?

SOLUTION

Step 1: List the given and unknown values.

> **Given:** *mechanical advantage* = 2.2
>
> *output distance* = 0.45 m
>
> **Unknown:** *input distance* = ? m

Step 2: Write the mechanical advantage equation, and rearrange it to solve for input distance. Because the given information involves only distance, only the second form of the equation is needed.

$$mechanical\ advantage = \frac{input\ distance}{output\ distance}$$

$$mechanical\ advantage \times output\ distance$$

$$= \frac{input\ distance \times \cancel{output\ distance}}{\cancel{output\ distance}} = input\ distance$$

Step 3: Insert the known values into the equation, and solve.

$$input\ distance = 2.2 \times 0.45\ m$$

$$input\ distance = 0.99\ m$$

PRACTICE

1. If an input force of 202 N is applied to the handles of the wheelbarrow in the sample problem, how large is the output force that just lifts the load?

   _____

2. Suppose you need to remove a nail from a board by using a claw hammer. What is the input distance for a claw hammer if the output distance is 2.0 cm and the mechanical advantage is 5.5?

   _____

PROBLEM

A lever and fulcrum are used to raise a heavy rock, which has a weight of 445 N. If the lever has a mechanical advantage of 9.50, what must the input force on the lever be in order to just begin lifting the rock?

SOLUTION

Step 1: List the given and unknown values.

> **Given:** *mechanical advantage* = 9.50
>
> *output force* = 445 N
>
> **Unknown:** *input force* = ? N

Step 2: Write the mechanical advantage equation, and rearrange it to solve for input force. Because the given information involves only force, only the first form of the equation is needed.

$$mechanical\ advantage = \frac{output\ force}{input\ force}$$

$$input\ force \times mechanical\ advantage = \frac{output\ force}{\cancel{input\ force}} \times \cancel{input\ force}$$

$$\frac{input\ force \times \cancel{mechanical\ advantage}}{\cancel{mechanical\ advantage}} = \frac{output\ force}{mechanical\ advantage}$$

Step 3: Insert the known values into the equation, and solve.

$$input\ force = \frac{445\ N}{9.50}$$

$$input\ force = 46.8\ N$$

PRACTICE

3. An axe is driven into a piece of wood a distance of 3.0 cm. If the mechanical advantage of the axe is 0.85, how far is the wood split?

_____

4. The mechanical advantage of a wheel and axle is 8.93×10^{-2}. If the wheel's output force is 2.22×10^3 N, what is the input force that turns the axle?

_____

5. An Archimedean screw is a screw within a closely fitting cover, so that water can be raised when the screw is turned. The screw has a mechanical advantage of 12.5. If the screw is turned several times, so that the input distance is 1.57 m, how much water has been lifted upward by the screw?

_____

| Math Skills *continued*

PROBLEM

A pulley is used to raise a heavy crate. The pulley is such that an input force of 223 N is needed to provide an output force of 1,784 N. What is the mechanical advantage of this pulley?

SOLUTION

Step 1: **List the given and unknown values.**

Given: *output force* = 1,784 N

input force = 223 N

Unknown: *mechanical advantage* = ?

Step 2: **Write the mechanical advantage equation.** Because the given information involves only force, only the first form of the equation is needed.

$$mechanical\ advantage = \frac{output\ force}{input\ force}$$

Step 3: **Insert the known values into the equation, and solve.**

$$mechanical\ advantage = \frac{1784\ N}{223\ N}$$

$$mechanical\ advantage = 8.00$$

PRACTICE

6. A mover uses a ramp to load a crate of nails onto a truck. The crate, which must be lifted 1.4 m from the street to the bed of the truck, is pushed along the length of the ramp. If the ramp is 4.6 m long and friction between the ramp and crate can be ignored, what is the mechanical advantage of the ramp?

_____

7. A complex arrangement of pulleys forms what is called the block in a block and tackle. The rope used to lift the pulleys and the load is the tackle. A block and tackle is used to lift a truck engine, which weighs nearly 7,406 N. The force required to lift this weight using the block and tackle is 308.6 N. What is the mechanical advantage of the block and tackle?

_____

8. If you try opening a door by pushing too close to the side where the hinges are, you may find it difficult to push open. Suppose you are trying to open a door that is 85 cm wide. If you push on the door at a point 15 cm away from the hinges, what is the mechanical advantage?

_____

MIXED PRACTICE

9. It has been proposed that the stones of the Pyramids in Egypt were raised by using ramps. Suppose one of these ramps had a mechanical advantage of 3.86. If an input force of 6,350 N was provided by laborers, what would the output force on the stone have been?

_____

10. A wedge with a mechanical advantage of 0.78 is used to raise a house corner from its foundation. If the output force is 7,500 N, what is the input force?

_____

11. A pennyfarthing is a style of bicycle with a very large front wheel and a small rear wheel. The cyclist, who sits high above and behind the front wheel, pedals this wheel directly. The distance the pedals are turned (input distance) in one rotation is about 0.64 m. If the mechanical advantage of the pennyfarthing is 0.16, how far does the large wheel turn in one rotation?

_____

12. A block and tackle with a mechanical advantage of 48 is used to lift a piano 11 m to the third floor of a building. Although the arrangement of pulleys in the block and tackle makes it easy to lift the piano, it takes a long time because of the length of rope that must be pulled to lift the piano a small amount. What is this length, or input distance, of the rope that must be pulled?

_____

13. Archimedes is supposed to have said, "Give me a place to stand on and I will move the Earth." Suppose you had an object with a mass equal to that of Earth—5.98×10^{24} kg—and that it experienced gravity equal to that at Earth's surface, so that its weight was 5.87×10^{25} N. If by using a lever you could move this mass with a force of 175 N, what would be the mechanical advantage of the lever?

_____

14. Suppose the fulcrum of the lever in problem 13 is placed 1.00 m away from the mass. How far from the fulcrum would you have to be (what would the input distance be) in order for the lever to have the mechanical advantage you calculated in problem 13? (Note: the nearest galaxy to ours, the Andromeda Nebula, is 2 million light years, or 1.9×10^{22} m, away.)

_____

15. The input distance of a screw is equal to the circumference of the screw multiplied by the number of times it is turned. If a screw with a circumference of 19 mm is turned 4 times, so that it penetrates into a piece of wood a distance of 8.5 mm, what is the screw's mechanical advantage?

_____

Skills Worksheet

Math Skills

Gravitational Potential Energy

After you study each sample problem and solution, work out the practice problems on a separate sheet of paper. Write your answers in the spaces provided.

PROBLEM

An automobile to be transported by ship is raised 7.0 m above the dock. If its gravitational potential energy is 6.6×10^4 J, what is the automobile's mass?

SOLUTION

Step 1: List the given and unknown values.

Given: *gravitational potential energy, PE = 6.6×10^4 J*

height, h = 7.0 m

free-fall acceleration, g = 9.8 m/s²

Unknown: *mass, m = ? kg*

Step 2: Write the gravitational potential energy equation, and rearrange it to solve for mass.

gravitational potential energy =
mass × free-fall acceleration × height

$$PE = mgh$$

$$\frac{PE}{gh} = \frac{m\cancel{g}\cancel{h}}{\cancel{g}\cancel{h}} = m$$

Step 3: Insert the known values into the equation, and solve.

$$m = \frac{6.6 \times 10^4 \text{ J}}{9.8 \text{ m/s}^2 \times 7.0 \text{ m}} = \frac{6.6 \times 10^4 \text{ kg} \bullet \text{m}^2/\text{s}^2}{9.8 \text{ m/s}^2 \times 7.0 \text{ m}}$$

$$m = 9.6 \times 10^2 \text{ kg}$$

PRACTICE

1. The world record for pole vaulting is 6.15 m. If the pole vaulter's gravitational potential is 4,942 J, what is his mass?

_____

2. One of the tallest radio towers is in Fargo, North Dakota. The tower is 629 m tall, or about 44 percent taller than the Sears Tower in Chicago. If a bird lands on top of the tower, so that the gravitational potential energy associated with the bird is 2,033 J, what is its mass?

_____

Math Skills *continued*

PROBLEM

The largest sea turtle found in the United States had a mass of 860 kg. If the gravitational potential energy associated with the turtle, as it was being lifted onto a ship, was 2.0×10^4 J, how high above the water was the turtle?

SOLUTION

Step 1: **List the given and unknown values.**

> **Given:** *gravitational potential energy, PE $= 2.0 \times 10^4$ J*
> *mass, m $= 860$ kg*
> *free-fall acceleration, g $= 9.8$ m/s^2*

> **Unknown:** *height, h $= ?$ m*

Step 2: **Write the gravitational potential energy equation, and rearrange it to solve for height.**

> *gravitational potential energy =*
> *mass $\times$ free-fall acceleration $\times$ height*
>
> $PE = mgh$
>
> $\dfrac{PE}{mg} = \dfrac{\cancel{m}g h}{\cancel{m}g} = h$

Step 3: **Insert the known values into the equation, and solve.**

> $h = \dfrac{2.0 \times 10^4 \text{ J}}{860 \text{ kg} \times 9.8 \text{ m/s}^2} = \dfrac{2.0 \times 10^4 \text{ kg} \bullet \text{m}^2/\text{s}^2}{860 \text{ kg} \times 9.8 \text{ m/s}^2}$
>
> $h = 2.4$ m

PRACTICE

3. In 1993, Cuban athlete Javier Sotomayor set the world record for the high jump. The gravitational potential energy associated with Sotomayor's jump was 1,970 J. Sotomayor's mass was 82.0 kg. How high did Sotomayor jump?

_____

4. A 1,750 kg weather satellite moves in a circular orbit with a gravitational potential energy of 1.69×10^{10} J. At its location, free-fall acceleration is only 6.44 m/s^2. How high above Earth's surface is the satellite?

_____

| Math Skills *continued*

PROBLEM

What is the gravitational potential energy associated with a 75 kg tourist at the top floor of the Sears Tower in Chicago, with respect to the street 436 m below?

SOLUTION

Step 1:   List the given and unknown values.

> **Given:**   *mass, m* = 75 kg
>
> *height, h* = 436 m
>
> *free-fall acceleration, g* = 9.8 m/s^2

Unknown: *gravitational potential energy, PE* = ? J

Step 2:   Write the equation for gravitational potential energy.

> *gravitational potential energy =*
> *mass × free-fall acceleration × height*
>
> *PE = mgh*

Step 3: Insert the known values into the equation, and solve.

> $PE = (75 \text{ kg}) \times (9.8 \text{ m/s}^2) \times (436 \text{ m}) = 3.2 \times 10^5 \text{ kg} \cdot \text{m}^2/\text{s}^2$
>
> $PE = 3.2 \times 10^5 \text{ J}$

PRACTICE

5. With an elevation of 5,334 m above sea level, the village of Aucanquilca, Chile is the highest inhabited town in the world. What would be the gravitational potential energy associated with a 64 kg person in Aucanquilca?

_____

6. The peak of the extinct volcano Volcán Chimborazo in Ecuador is the farthest point on Earth from Earth's center. This is because Earth bulges outward due to its rotation, and this bulge is greatest at the Equator, which is only about 100 km north of Chimborazo. Volcán Chimborazo's summit is 6,267 m above sea level. If a mountain climber with a mass of 85 kg (climbing equipment included) reaches the mountain's peak, what is the gravitational potential energy associated with the climber with respect to sea level?

_____

MIXED PRACTICE

7. The Royal Gorge Bridge is situated 321 m above the Arkansas River in Colorado. If the gravitational potential energy associated with a tourist on the bridge is 1.73×10^5 J with respect to the river, what is the tourist's mass?

_____

Skills Worksheet

Math Skills

Kinetic Energy

After you study each sample problem and solution, work out the practice problems on a separate sheet of paper. Write your answers in the spaces provided.

PROBLEM

A 725 kg automobile has a kinetic energy of J as it travels along a highway. What is the car's speed?

SOLUTION

Step 1: List the given and unknown values.

        Given: *mass, m* = 725 kg

                    kinetic energy, KE = 3.02×10^5

      Unknown: *speed, v* = ? m/s

Step 2: Write the kinetic energy equation, and rearrange it to solve for speed.

$$kinetic\ energy = \frac{1}{2} \times mass \times speed\ squared \qquad\qquad KE = \frac{1}{2}mv^2$$

$$KE \times \frac{2}{m} = \frac{1}{2}mv^2 \times \left(\frac{2}{m}\right) = v^2$$

$$v = \sqrt{v^2} = \sqrt{\frac{2KE}{m}}$$

Step 3: Insert the known values into the equation, and solve.

$$v = \sqrt{\frac{2(3.02 \times 10^5\ \text{J})}{725\ \text{kg}}} = \sqrt{\frac{2(3.02 \times 10^5\ \text{kg} \cdot \text{m}^2/\text{s}^2)}{725\ \text{kg}}}$$

$$v = 28.9\ \text{m/s}$$

PRACTICE

1. When a 65 kg skydiver jumps from a plane, her speed steadily increases until air resistance provides a force that balances the force due to free fall. How fast is the skydiver falling if her kinetic energy at the moment is 7.04×10^5 J?

_____

2. The kinetic energy of a golf ball is measured to be 143.3 J. If the golf ball has a mass of about 47 g, what is its speed?

_____

PROBLEM

The greatest speed that a meteoroid can have and still be pulled down to Earth's surface is 70.0 km/s. If a meteoroid traveling with this speed has a kinetic energy of 2.56×10^{13} J, what is its mass?

SOLUTION

Step 1: **List the given and unknown values.**

Given: *speed,* $v = 70.0$ km/s $= 7.00 \times 10^4$ m/s

kinetic energy, $KE = 2.56 \times 10^{13}$ J

Unknown: *mass,* $m = ?$ kg

Step 2: **Write the kinetic energy equation, and rearrange it to solve for mass.**

$$kinetic\ energy = \frac{1}{2} \times mass \times speed\ squared \qquad KE = \frac{1}{2}mv^2$$

$$KE \times \left(\frac{2}{v^2}\right) = \frac{1}{2}mv^2 \times \left(\frac{2}{v^2}\right) = m$$

Step 3: **Insert the known values into the equation, and solve.**

$$m = \frac{2 \times (2.56 \times 10^{13}\ J)}{(7.00 \times 10^4\ m/s)^2} = \frac{2 \times (2.56 \times 10^{13}\ kg \cdot m^2/s^2)}{(7.00 \times 10^4\ m/s)^2}$$

$$m = 1.04 \times 10^4\ kg$$

PRACTICE

3. The most massive Shinkansen bullet trains are the series-200 trains. This type of train also has one of the highest operating speeds: 76.4 m/s. If a series-200 train has a maximum kinetic energy of 2.78×10^9 J, what is its mass?

_____

4. The largest airplane built that has flown more than once is the Ukrainian-built Antonov-225 *Mriya*. With a length of 85 m and a wingspan of 88 m, the *Mriya (Dream)* was designed to carry the space shuttle of the Soviet Union's space program. Unloaded, the top speed of *Mriya* is 236 m/s, at which its kinetic energy is 9.76×10^9 J. What is its mass?

_____

5. The vehicle land-speed record has long been held by rocket cars. These vehicles resemble the high-speed rocket planes that were used in the early days of the space program, but they have heavy metal wheels. On September 5, 1997, the world land-speed record was set by the British-built Thrust SSC rocket car, which had a top recorded speed of 341 m/s. The kinetic energy of the car at this speed is 5.289×10^8 J. What is the car's mass?

_____

| Math Skills *continued* |

PROBLEM

A baseball is pitched with a speed of 35 m/s. If the baseball has a mass of 0.146 kg, what is its kinetic energy?

SOLUTION

Step 1: List the given and unknown values.

Given: *mass, m* = 0.146 kg

   speed, v = 35 m/s

Unknown: *kinetic energy, KE* = ? J

Step 2: Write the equation for kinetic energy.

$$kinetic\ energy = \frac{1}{2} \times mass \times speed\ squared \qquad\qquad KE = \frac{1}{2}mv^2$$

Step 3: Insert the known values into the kinetic energy equation, and solve.

$$KE = \frac{1}{2}(0.146\ \text{kg}) \times (35\ \text{m/s})^2 = 89\ \text{kg} \cdot \text{m}^2/\text{s}^2$$

$$KE = 89\ \text{J}$$

PRACTICE

6. A cheetah can run briefly with a speed of 31 m/s. Suppose a cheetah with a mass of 47 kg runs at this speed. What is the cheetah's kinetic energy?

_____

7. A table tennis (ping-pong) ball has a mass of about 2.45 g. Suppose the ball is hit across the table with a speed of about 4.0 m/s. What is its kinetic energy?

_____

MIXED PRACTICE

8. The largest land predator is the male polar bear, which typically has a mass of around 5.00×10^2 kg. If the maximum kinetic energy for a polar bear with this mass is 6.05×10^4 J, what is its top speed?

_____

9. Though slow on land, the leatherback turtle holds the record for the fastest water speed of any reptile: 9.78 m/s. It is also among the largest of reptiles. Suppose the largest leatherback yet discovered were to swim at a speed of 9.78 m/s. If its kinetic energy was 6.08×10^4 J, what was its mass?

_____

Skills Worksheet

Math Skills

Efficiency

After you study each sample problem and solution, work out the practice problems on a separate sheet of paper. Write your answers in the spaces provided.

PROBLEM

A diesel engine with an efficiency of 0.39 requires 750 J of work to be done on its pistons. How much useful work is done by the diesel engine?

SOLUTION

Step 1: List the given and unknown values.

> **Given:** *efficiency* = 0.39
>
> *work input* = 750 J
>
> **Unknown:** *useful work output* = ? J

Step 2: Write the efficiency equation, and rearrange it to solve for useful work output.

$$efficiency = \frac{useful\ work\ output}{work\ input}$$

$$efficiency \times work\ input$$

$$= \frac{useful\ work\ output}{work\ input}$$

$$\times work\ input$$

$$= useful\ work\ output$$

Step 3: Insert the known values into the equation, and solve.

$$useful\ work\ output = (0.39) \times (750\ J)$$

$$useful\ work\ output = 290\ J$$

PRACTICE

1. The resistance of water to an oar in a rowboat limits the oar's efficiency to 0.450. If the rower does 145 J of work on the oar with each stroke, how much useful work is done by the oar?

_____

2. A jack requires 808 J of work to be done in raising a load, and ideally would do this amount of useful work. However, internal friction reduces the jack's efficiency to 0.625. How much useful work is done by the jack?

_____

| Math Skills *continued*

PROBLEM

A block and tackle does 1.25×10^5 J of useful work, but friction limits the block and tackle to an efficiency of 0.45. What is the amount of work that must be done on the block and tackle?

SOLUTION

Step 1: List the given and unknown values.

> **Given:** *efficiency* = 0.45
>
> *useful work output* = 1.25×10^5 J
>
> **Unknown:** *work input* = ? J

Step 2: Use the efficiency equation, and rearrange it to solve for work input.

$$efficiency = \frac{useful\ work\ output}{work\ input}$$

$$efficiency \times \frac{work\ input}{efficiency}$$

$$= \frac{useful\ work\ output}{work\ input}$$

$$\times \frac{work\ input}{efficiency}$$

$$work\ input = \frac{useful\ work\ output}{efficiency}$$

Step 3: Substitute the values for the useful work done by the machine and the efficiency into the equation, and solve.

$$work\ input = \frac{1.25 \times 10^5\ J}{0.45}$$

$$work\ input = 2.8 \times 10^5\ J$$

PRACTICE

3. An automobile gasoline engine is able to do 225 J of useful work with each stroke of its pistons. If the engine has an efficiency of 29.0 percent, what is the amount of work that must be done on the pistons in the engine?

_____

4. The most efficient type of steam engine is a steam turbine, which in practice can have an efficiency as high as 30.0 percent. If the useful work done each second by a steam turbine with this efficiency is 2.64×10^6 J, how much work must the steam do on the turbine?

_____

PROBLEM

An inclined plane allows you to do 280 J of useful work on a refrigerator that you are sliding upward along the plane. If the work that you have to do is 760 J, what is the efficiency of the plane?

SOLUTION

Step 1: **List the given and unknown values.**

Given: *work input* = 760 J

useful work output = 280 J

Unknown: *efficiency* = ?

Step 2: **Write the equation for efficiency.**

$$efficiency = \frac{useful\ work\ output}{work\ input}$$

Step 3: **Insert the known values into the equation, and solve.**

$$efficiency = \frac{280\ J}{760\ J} = 0.37$$

To express this as a percentage, multiply by 100 and add the percent sign, "%."

$$efficiency = 0.37 \times 100 = 37\%$$

PRACTICE

5. A forklift developed in Sweden is able to do 1.8×10^6 J of useful work in lifting a heavy load. Suppose 7.6×10^6 J must be done by the lift's motors on the load in order to accomplish this task. What is the efficiency of the forklift?

_____

MIXED PRACTICE

6. A steam engine does 2,500 J of useful work to move a wheel through half a rotation. The energy provided to the steam engine by heat for this work equals 7,576 J. Noting that the amount of energy provided to a machine, either by heat or by work, is equivalent to the amount of work that must be done on a machine, calculate the efficiency of the engine.

_____

7. A pennyfarthing bicycle has an efficiency of 62 percent. How much work is done by the bicycle if a cyclist does 5.4×10^3 J of work on the bicycle?

_____

Skills Worksheet

Math Skills

Temperature Conversions

After you study each sample problem and solution, work out the practice problems on a separate sheet of paper. Write your answers in the space provided.

PROBLEM

Earth's moon rotates about once every 29 days, so that day and night on the moon last about two weeks each. The moon's surface can reach a daytime temperature of 117°C. What is this temperature in degrees Fahrenheit and kelvins?

SOLUTION

Step 1: **List the given and unknown values.**

Given: $t = 117$°C

Unknown: $T_F = ?$ °F, $T = ?$ K

Step 2: **Write down the equations for temperature conversions.**

$$T_F = 1.8\,t + 32.0$$
$$T = t + 273$$

Step 3: **Insert the known values into the equations, and solve.**

$$T_F = (1.8 \times 117) + 32.0 = 211 + 32.0 = 243°F$$
$$T = 117 + 273 = 3.90 \times 10^2 \text{ K}$$

PRACTICE

1. The highest surface temperature on any of the solar system's planets is found on Venus. Partly because of its nearness to the sun and partly because of the extreme pressure of its atmosphere, the average daytime temperature on Venus is 453°C. What is this temperature in degrees Fahrenheit and in kelvins?

_____

2. In contrast to Venus, the coldest temperature yet measured on the surface of any body in the solar system is –235°C. This temperature was detected by *Voyager 2* as it passed by Neptune's largest moon, Triton. What is Triton's surface temperature in degrees Fahrenheit and in kelvins?

_____

3. The warmest temperature in Antarctica was recorded at the Vanda Station on the Scott Coast. On January 5, 1974—early summer in the southern hemisphere—a high temperature of 15°C was reached. Express this temperature in degrees Fahrenheit and kelvins.

4. A recipe for bread states that the dough must bake for 40 minutes at a temperature of 190°C. The oven you are using has temperature markings on the dial that are in units of degrees Fahrenheit. At what Fahrenheit temperature must the bread be baked? What would this temperature be in kelvins?

PROBLEM

The lowest temperature on the moon's surface occurs during the two weeks that make up a lunar night. This low temperature is –261.4°F. What is this temperature in degrees Celsius and kelvins?

SOLUTION

Step 1: **List the given and unknown values.**

Given: $T_F = -261.4°F$

Unknown: $t = ? °C, T = ? K$

Step 2: **Write down the equations for temperature conversions.**

$$t = \frac{(T_F - 32.0)}{1.8}$$

$$T = t + 273$$

Step 3: **Insert the known values into equations, and solve.**

$$t = \frac{(-261.4 - 32.0)}{1.8} = \frac{-293.4}{1.8} = -163.0°C$$

$$T = -163.0 + 273 = 1.10 \times 10^2 \, K$$

PRACTICE

5. Hot water heaters often have warning labels indicating that injuries can result when the temperature of the water is above 125°F. What is this temperature in degrees Celsius and in kelvins?

6. Only three times in the history of weather monitoring in the United States have the national high and low temperatures for one day occurred in the same location. On November 11, 1911, in Oklahoma City, the low temperature was 17°F and the high temperature was 83°F, a difference of 66 Fahrenheit degrees. What were these high and low temperatures in degrees Celsius and kelvins?

7. Antifreeze is able to work because its freezing point is lower than that of water. Water and antifreeze combined together have an even lower freezing point. A mixture of two-thirds antifreeze and one-third water freezes at –83.9°F. What is this temperature in degrees Celsius and in kelvins?

8. Most antifreezes also serve as engine coolants, because their boiling points are higher than that of water. Water and antifreeze combined together have an even higher boiling point. A mixture of two-thirds antifreeze/coolant and one-third water boils at 276°F. What is this temperature in degrees Celsius and in kelvins?

PROBLEM

Oxygen freezes under atmospheric pressure at a temperature of 54.4 K. What is this temperature in degrees Celsius and degrees Fahrenheit?

SOLUTION

Step 1: List the given and unknown values.

> **Given:** $T = 54.4$ K
>
> **Unknown:** $t = ?$ °C, $T_F = ?$ °F

Step 2: Write down the equations for temperature conversions.

> $T = t + 273$
>
> $T_F = 1.8\,t + 32.0$

Step 3: Insert the known values into the equations and solve.

> $t = T - 273$
> $t = 54.4 - 273 = -218.6$°C
>
> $t = -219$°C
>
> $T_F = 1.8(-219) + 32.0 = -394 + 32$
>
> $T_F = -362$°F

Name_____ Class _____ Date _____

Math Skills *continued*

PRACTICE

9. The temperature at Earth's center is estimated to be about 5,100 K. Express this temperature in both degrees Celsius and degrees Fahrenheit.

10. One of the most deadly features of an erupting volcano is an avalanche of hot ash and gas called a *pyroclastic flow*. A pyroclastic flow can move at a speed of over 160 km/h and can have a temperature of 1,088 K. What is this temperature in degrees Fahrenheit and degrees Celsius?

11. The coolest part of the sun is the region called the *chromosphere,* which is the region above the sun's apparent surface, or *photosphere.* At 1,100 km above the photosphere, the temperature of the chromosphere is about 3,500 K. What is this temperature in degrees Fahrenheit and degrees Celsius?

12. The highest temperature that the atmosphere of Mars reaches is about 240 K. What is this temperature in degrees Fahrenheit and degrees Celsius?

MIXED PRACTICE

13. One of the most dramatic temperature changes over a short distance occurs in Ecuador. The average temperature at the town of Ventanas, which is at 100 m above sea level, is 29°C. Some 70 km to the east is the extinct volcano, Volcán Chimborazo, the summit of which is 6,270 m above sea level. The temperature at the summit is 11°C, in spite of the mountain being only about 170 km south of the equator. Express both temperatures in degrees Fahrenheit.

14. The sun's temperature decreases steadily as the distance from its innermost regions increases. The sole exception to this is in the outermost part of the sun's atmosphere. This region, called the *corona,* consists of thin gases that are heated by the sun's magnetic field. As a result, the corona has an average temperature of about 1.0×10^6 K. What is this temperature in degrees Celsius?

15. Liquid helium has the lowest boiling point of any liquid at atmospheric pressure. Helium remains in the gaseous state until its temperature is lowered to 4.25 K, at which point it condenses into a liquid state. Express the boiling point of liquid helium in degrees Fahrenheit.

| Math Skills *continued*

16. One of the most rapid increases in temperature occurred on January 22, 1943, in the town of Spearfish, South Dakota. Within 2 minutes, the temperature increased 49°F.

    a. What was the change in temperature in degrees Celsius?

    _____

    b. The temperature of the air after the 2 minutes had passed was 45°F. What was the starting temperature in degrees Fahrenheit?

    _____

    c. What were the starting and final temperatures in degrees Celsius?

    _____

17. The electric heating element on a stove uses electricity to raise its temperature. A typical heating element can reach a temperature of about 4,200°C. Express this temperature in kelvins.

    _____

18. *Hypothermia* is a condition in which the body gives up too much heat energy to its colder surroundings. For humans, a drop in body temperature to 90.0°F can cause unconsciousness, and a temperature of 78°F can be fatal.

    a. Express these temperatures in degrees Celsius.

    _____

    b. In one recent case, a young girl was accidentally locked out of her home during winter. When she was discovered, her body temperature had fallen to 14°C. Fortunately, she survived and recovered fully. What was her body temperature in degrees Fahrenheit? How much lower is this temperature than the normal fatal temperature for hypothermia?

    _____

19. Just as the human body cannot survive if its temperature falls too low, it also cannot survive if its temperature is too high. In a condition called *hyperthermia,* energy is transferred to the body from its surroundings, causing the body's temperature to increase. The condition known as *heat stroke* is a severe form of hyperthermia. Normally, a person cannot survive for long at a temperature of about 42°C, although a recent survivor of heat stroke had a high temperature of nearly 47°C. Express both of these temperatures in degrees Fahrenheit.

    _____

Skills Worksheet

Math Skills

Specific Heat

After you study each sample problem and solution, work out the practice problems on a separate sheet of paper. Write your answers in the space provided.

PROBLEM

Lithium has the highest specific heat of any pure metal. The temperature of a 25.00 g sample of lithium will increase by 7.69 K when 684.4 J of energy is added to it. What is lithium's specific heat?

SOLUTION

Step 1: List the given and unknown values.

Given: $\Delta t = 7.69$ K

$m = 25.00$ g $= 25.00 \times 10^{-3}$ kg

$energy = 684.4$ J

Unknown: $c = ?$ J/kg • K

Step 2: Write down the specific heat equation, and rearrange it to solve for specific heat.

$$energy = cm\Delta t$$

$$\frac{energy}{m\Delta t} = \frac{cm\Delta t}{m\Delta t}$$

$$c = \frac{energy}{m\Delta t}$$

Step 3: Substitute the energy, mass, and temperature change values, and solve.

$$c = \left(\frac{684.4 \text{ J}}{(25.00 \times 10^{-3} \text{ kg}) \times 7.69 \text{ K}} \right)$$

$$c = 3,560 \text{ J/kg} \cdot \text{K}$$

PRACTICE

1. Brass is an alloy made from copper and zinc. A 0.59 kg brass candlestick has an initial temperature of 98.0°C. If 2.11×10^4 J of energy is removed from the candlestick to lower its temperature to 6.8°C, what is the specific heat of brass?

2. Mercury has one of the lowest specific heats. This fact added to its liquid state at most atmospheric temperatures makes it effective for use in thermometers. If 257 J of energy are added to 0.450 kg of mercury, the mercury's temperature will increase by 4.09 K. What is the specific heat of mercury?

_____

3. A 0.38 kg drinking glass is filled with a hot liquid. The liquid transfers 7,032 J of energy to the glass. If the temperature of the glass increases by 22 K, what is the specific heat of the glass?

_____

PROBLEM

The water in a swimming pool gives up 1.09×10^{10} J of energy to the cool night air. If the temperature of the water, which has a specific heat of 4,186 J/kg • K, decreases by 5.0 K, what is the mass of the water in the pool?

SOLUTION

Step 1: **List the given and unknown values.**

Given: *energy* $= 1.09 \times 10^{10}$ J

$c = 4,186$ J/kg • K

$\Delta t = 5.0$ K

Unknown: $m = ?$ kg

Step 2: **Write down the specific heat equation, and rearrange it to solve for mass.**

$$energy = cm\Delta t$$

$$\frac{energy}{c\Delta t} = \frac{cm\Delta t}{c\Delta t}$$

$$m = \frac{energy}{c\Delta t}$$

Step 3: **Substitute the energy, specific heat, and temperature change values, and solve.**

$$m = \left| \frac{1.09 \times 10^{10} \text{ J}}{\left(4,186 \text{J/kg} \bullet \text{K}\right) \times 5.0 \text{K}} \right|$$

$$m = 5.2 \times 10^{5} \text{ kg}$$

PRACTICE

4. Bismuth's specific heat is 121 J/kg • K, the lowest of any non-radioactive metal. What is the mass of a bismuth sample if 25 J raises its temperature 5.0 K?

_____

| Math Skills *continued*

5. The temperature of air in a foundry increases when molten metals cool and solidify. Suppose 9.9×10^6 J of energy is added to the surrounding air by the solidifying metal. The air's temperature increases by 55 K, and the air has a specific heat capacity of 1.0×10^3 J/kg • K.

   a. What is the mass of the heated air?

   _____

   b. Assuming a density of 1.29 kg/m³, what is the heated air's volume?

   _____

6. The temperature of air above coastal areas is greatly influenced by the large specific heat of water. The specific heat of air between temperatures of 40°F and 90°F is about 1,000.0 J/kg • K. Consider the situation where 4,186 J of energy is given up by 1.0 kg of water, causing its temperature to drop by 1.0 K.

   a. If the air over the water increases temperature by 5.5 K, what is its mass?

   _____

   b. What is the volume of the air over the water, assuming that the air's density is 1.29 kg/m³?

   _____

PROBLEM

A 0.150 kg iron bolt is heated by 1.245×10^4 J of energy. If the bolt, which has a specific heat of 448 J/kg • K, reaches a temperature of 455 K after heating, what was its initial temperature?

SOLUTION

Step 1: List the given and unknown values.

   Given: $m = 0.150$ kg

   $energy = 1.245 \times 10^4$ J

   $c = 448$ J/kg • K

   $final\ T = 455$ K

   Unknown: *initial T* = ? K

Step 2: Rearrange the specific heat equation to solve for initial temperature.

$$energy = cm\Delta t$$

$$\frac{energy}{cm} = \frac{cm\Delta t}{cm}$$

$$\Delta t = final\ T - initial\ T = \frac{energy}{cm}$$

$$initial\ T = final\ T - \frac{energy}{cm}$$

Step 3: **Substitute the specific heat, mass, and energy values, and solve.**

$$initial\ T = 455\ K - \left(\frac{1.245 \times 10^4\ J}{(448\ J/kg \cdot K) \times 0.150\ kg}\right) = 455\ K - 185\ K$$

$$initial\ T = 2.7 \times 10^2\ K$$

PRACTICE

7. A 0.190 kg piece of copper is heated and fashioned into a bracelet. The amount of energy transferred by heat to the copper is 6.62×10^4 J. If the specific heat of copper is 385 J/kg • K what is the change in the temperature of the copper?

_____

8. A 0.225 kg sample of tin, which has a specific heat of 2.3×10^2 J/kg • K, is cooled in water. The amount of energy transferred to the water is 3.9×10^3 J. If the final temperature of the tin is 18°C, what was its initial temperature?

_____

9. Tantalum is an element that is used, among other things, in making aircraft parts. Suppose the properties of a tantalum part are being tested at high temperatures. Tantalum has a specific heat of about 140 J/kg • K. The aircraft part has a mass of 0.23 kg and is cooled from a temperature of 1,200 K by being placed in water. If 3.0×10^4 J of energy is transferred to the water, what is the final temperature of the part?

_____

PROBLEM

A cup is made of an experimental material that can hold hot liquids without significantly increasing its own temperature. The cup's mass is 0.75 kg, and its specific heat is 1,860 J/kg • K. If the temperature of the cup increases from 20.0°C to 36.5°C, what is the amount of energy that has been transferred by heat into the cup?

SOLUTION

Step 1: **List the given and unknown values.**

> **Given:** $t = 36.5°C - 20.0°\ C = 16.5°\ C = 16.5\ K$
>
> $m = 0.75\ kg$
>
> $c = 1,860\ J/kg \cdot K$
>
> **Unknown:** *energy* = ?

Step 2: **Write out the equation for specific heat.**

> $$energy = cm\Delta t$$

Step 3: Substitute the specific heat, mass, and temperature change values, and solve.

$$energy = \left(\frac{1{,}860\,J}{kg\bullet K}\right) \times (0.75\ kg) \times (16.5\ K)$$

$$energy = 2.3 \times 10^4\ J = 23\ kJ$$

PRACTICE

10. The element hydrogen has the highest specific heat of all elements. At a temperature of 25°C, hydrogen's specific heat is 1.43×10^4 J/kg • K. If the temperature of a 0.34 kg sample of hydrogen is to be raised by 25 K, how much energy will have to be added to the hydrogen?

_____

11. The element radon is at the opposite end of the range with the lowest specific heat of all naturally occurring elements. At 25°C, radon's specific heat is 94 J/kg • K. If the temperature of a 0.34 kg sample of radon is to be raised by 25 K, how much energy will have to be added to the radon?

_____

12. The soup in a bowl is too hot to eat, so you need to find some way to cool it quickly. Although there are no ice cubes in the freezer, there are several stainless steel spoons that have been stored in the freezer for several hours. By placing the cold spoons in the bowl of hot soup, the soup's temperature is lowered from a temperature of 82°C to 48°C. The mass of the soup is 0.10 kg, while the mass of each spoon is 0.04 kg.

 a. Assuming the soup has the same specific heat as water (4,186 J/kg • K), how much energy is removed from the soup?

_____

 b. If the initial temperature of the spoons is –15°C and their specific heat is the same as iron, how many spoons are needed to cool the soup?

_____

MIXED PRACTICE

13. The technique known as *calorimetry* allows you to measure how much energy is added to or removed from a substance by heat. By placing the substance in a known quantity of water, which has a specific heat of 4,186 J/kg • K, and measuring the change in the water's temperature, the amount of energy added to or removed from the water can be determined. If the initial temperature and mass of the substance are also known, the substance's specific heat can also be determined. Suppose calorimetry is used to measure the energy given up by a hot piece of metal that is submerged in 1.5 kg of water. If the energy added to the water equals 3.14×10^4 J, how much does the water's temperature increase?

_____

| Math Skills *continued*

14. A ring with a mass of 25.5 g appears to be pure silver. Rather than test for density, you can confirm the ring's composition by determining its specific heat. Suppose the ring is heated to a temperature of 84.0°C and then immersed in a container of water until the ring's temperature is 25.0°C. If the ring gives up 667.5 J of energy to the water, what is its specific heat? Is the ring made of silver ($c = 234$ J/kg • K), nickel ($c = 444$ J/kg • K), or palladium ($c = 244$ J/kg • K)?

_____

15. Beryllium is used for making rocket parts because of its light weight and sturdiness. It also has a high specific heat that is second among pure metals only to lithium. This specific heat, which is 1,825 J/kg • K, gives beryllium a high resistance to temperature change. Suppose a beryllium rocket component with a mass of 1.4 kg is tested at a high temperature and then cooled to 300.0 K. If the energy given up by the component is 2.555×10^6 J, what was its initial temperature?

_____

16. Of the four bodies of water on Earth that are called oceans, the smallest by far is the Arctic Ocean, which surrounds the North Pole. The Arctic Ocean is also the only large body of water in the world with a surface that is frozen throughout the year. The liquid water that lies beneath the layer of ice has a mass of about 1.33×10^{19} kg and a temperature of 4.00°C. Suppose 4.20×10^{17} J, which is the energy produced in one year by one of the world's largest power plants, is added to the Arctic Ocean. Assuming that the ocean's water has a heat capacity of 4,186 J/kg • K, what will the water's final temperature be?

_____

17. The planet Jupiter consists mostly of gases. Even the surface that appears as dark bands in photographs is a dense gas of mostly hydrogen and helium. The lighter bands of frozen ammonia (NH_3) lie 50 km above the dense surface gases. Although these clouds are only about 5 km thick and appear to cover about half of the planet's surface area, they have a volume of about 1.6×10^{11} km^3. Assume that the density of these clouds is 0.77 kg/m^3 and that the specific heat of ammonia ice is the same as ammonia gas (2.1×10^3 J/kg • K). If the temperature of these clouds increases by 1.0 K, how much energy will they have absorbed?

_____

18. When a driver brakes an automobile, friction between the brake disks and the brake pads converts part of the car's kinetic energy to energy that is transferred to the pads and disks by heat. During braking, 1.92×10^5 J of energy is added to each wheel's disk and brake pads, increasing temperature by 122 K. If the combined mass of each brake and its pads is 3.5 kg, what is their specific heat?

_____

Skills Worksheet

Math Skills

Wave Speed

After you study each sample problem and solution, work out the practice problems on a separate sheet of paper. Write your answers in the spaces provided.

PROBLEM

The musical note A above middle C has a frequency of 440 Hz. If the speed of sound is known to be 350 m/s, what is the wavelength of this note?

SOLUTION

Step 1: List the given and unknown values.

> **Given:** frequency, $f = 440$ Hz
>
> wave speed, $v = 350$ m/s
>
> **Unknown:** wavelength, $\lambda = ?$ m

Step 2: Write the equation for wave speed, and rearrange it to solve for wavelength.

$$v = f \times \lambda \qquad \lambda = \frac{v}{f}$$

Step 3: Insert the known values into the equation, and solve.

$$\lambda = \frac{350 \text{ m/s}}{440 \text{ Hz}}$$

$$\lambda = 0.80 \text{ m}$$

PRACTICE

1. A certain FM radio station broadcasts electromagnetic waves at a frequency of 9.05×107 Hz. These radio waves travel at a speed of 3.00×108 m/s. What is the wavelength of these radio waves?

_____

2. A dog whistle is designed to produce a sound with a frequency beyond that which can be heard by humans (between 20,000 Hz and 27,000 Hz). If a particular whistle produces a sound with a frequency of 2.5×104 Hz, what is the sound's wavelength? Assume the speed of sound in air is 331 m/s.

_____

Name_____ Class _____ Date _____

Math Skills *continued*

3. The lowest pitch that the average human can hear has a frequency of 20.0 Hz. What is the wavelength of a 20.0 Hz wave with a speed of 331 m/s?

_____

4. A 10.0 m wire is hung from a high ceiling and held tightly below by a large mass. Standing waves are created in the wire by air currents that pass over the wire, setting it in motion. If the speed of the standing wave is 335 m/s and its frequency is 67 Hz, what is its wavelength?

_____

5. Sonar is a device that uses reflected sound waves to measure underwater depths. If a sonar signal has a frequency of 288 Hz and the speed of sound in water is 1.45 × 103 m/s, what is the wavelength of the sonar signal?

_____

PROBLEM

A buoy bobs up and down in the ocean. The waves have a wavelength of 2.5 m, and they pass the buoy at a speed of 4.0 m/s. What is the frequency of the waves? How much time does it take for one wave to pass under the buoy?

SOLUTION

Step 1: List the given and unknown values.

    Given: wavelength, $\lambda = 2.5$ m

       wave speed, $v = 4.0$ m/s

   Unknown: frequency, $f = ?$ Hz

       period, $T = ?$ s

Step 2: Write the equation for wave speed, and rearrange it to solve for frequency. Write the equation for period.

$$v = f \times \lambda \qquad f = \frac{v}{\lambda}$$

$$T = \frac{1}{f}$$

Step 3: Insert the known values into the equations, and solve.

$$f = \frac{4.0 \text{ m/s}}{2.5 \text{ m}}$$

$$f = 1.6 \text{ Hz}$$

$$T = \frac{1}{1.6 \text{ Hz}}$$

$$T = 0.62 \text{ s}$$

Math Skills *continued*

PRACTICE

6. Cicadas produce a buzzing sound that has a wavelength in air of 2.69 m. If the speed of sound in air is 346 m/s, what is the frequency of the sound produced by a cicada? What is its period?

_____

7. A drum is struck, producing a wave with a wavelength of 110 cm and a speed of 2.42×104 m/s. What is the frequency of the wave? What is the period?

_____

8. One of the largest organ pipes is in the auditorium organ in the convention hall in Atlantic City, New Jersey. The pipe is 38.6 ft long and produces a sound with a wavelength of about 10.6 m. If the speed of sound in air is 346 m/s, what is the frequency of this sound?

_____

9. Yellow light with a wavelength of 5.89×10^{-7} m travels through quartz glass with a speed of 1.94×10^8 m/s. What is the frequency of the light?

_____

PROBLEM

Waves in a lake are 6 m apart and pass a person on a raft every 2 s. What is the speed of the waves?

SOLUTION

Step 1:   List the given and unknown values.

   Given: wavelength, $\lambda = 6$ m

                   period, $T = 2$ s

   Unknown: wave speed, $v = ?$ m/s

Step 2:   Write the equations for period and wave speed. Calculate the frequency from the period, and then determine the wave speed.

$$f = \frac{1}{T}$$

$$v = f \times \lambda$$

Step 3:   Insert the known values into the equations, and solve.

$$f = \frac{1}{2 \text{ s}} = 0.5 \text{ Hz}$$

$$v = (0.5 \text{ Hz}) \times (6 \text{ m})$$

$$v = 3 \text{ m/s}$$

Math Skills *continued*

PRACTICE

10. A wave with a frequency of 60.0 Hz travels through vulcanized rubber with a wavelength of 0.90 m. What is the speed of this wave?

_____

11. A wave with a frequency of 60.0 Hz travels through steel with a wavelength of 85.5 m. What is the speed of this wave?

_____

MIXED PRACTICE

12. Earthquakes generate shock waves that travel through Earth's interior to other parts of the world. The fastest of these waves are longitudinal waves, like sound waves, and are called *primary waves,* or just *p-waves.* A p-wave has a very low frequency, typically around 0.050 Hz. If the speed of a p-wave with this frequency is 8.0 km/s, what is its wavelength?

_____

13. Earthquakes also produce transverse waves that move more slowly than the p-waves. These waves are called *secondary waves*, or *s-waves*. If the wavelength of an s-wave is 2.3×10^4 m, and its speed is 4.5 km/s, what is its frequency?

_____

14. A dolphin can typically hear sounds with frequencies up to 150 kHz. What is the speed of sound in water if a wave with this frequency has a wavelength of 1.0 cm?

_____

15. A ship anchored at sea is rocked by waves that have crests 14 m apart. The waves travel at 7.0 m/s. How often do the wave crests reach the ship?

_____

Skills Worksheet

Math Skills

Resistance

After you study each sample problem and solution, work out the practice problems on a separate sheet of paper. Write your answers in the spaces provided.

PROBLEM

A clothes dryer is equipped with an electric heater. The heater works by passing air across an electric wire that is hot because of the current in it. The wire's resistance is 10.0 $|$, and the current in the wire equals 24 A. What is the voltage across the heater wire?

SOLUTION

Step 1: **List the given and unknown values.**

$\quad\quad$ **Given:** $\quad$ *resistance,* $R = 10.0\ |$

$\quad\quad\quad\quad\quad\quad$ *current,* $I = 24$ A

$\quad\quad$ **Unknown:** $\quad$ *voltage,* $V = ?$ V

Step 2. **Write the equation for resistance, and rearrange it to solve for voltage.**

$$R = \frac{V}{I} \quad\quad\quad\quad\quad\quad V = IR$$

Step 3. **Insert the known values into the equation, and solve.**

$$V = (10.0\ |) \times (24\ A)$$
$$V = 240\ V$$

PRACTICE

1. A hair dryer uses a wire that is hot because of the current in it to warm the air that blows through the dryer. The resistance of this wire is 7.7 $|$. If the current through the wire equals 15.6 A, what is the voltage across the terminals of the hair dryer?

_____

2. A battery-powered electric lantern is used as a light source for campers. The light bulb in the lantern has a resistance of 6.4 $|$. Assume the rest of the lantern's circuit has no resistance and that the current in the circuit is 0.75 A. Calculate the voltage across the terminals of the lantern's battery.

_____

Math Skills *continued*

3. Some kitchen sinks are equipped with electric garbage disposals. These are units with rapidly rotating steel blades that crush and chop food so that it can be washed down the drain instead of taking up space as solid garbage. The motor of a garbage disposal has a resistance of about 25.0 Ω. If the current in the motor is 4.66 A, what is the voltage across the motor's terminals?

_____

4. A washing machine motor works because of a current of 9.80 A in a circuit with a resistance of 12.2 Ω. What is the voltage across the terminals of the motor?

_____

5. A flashlight uses three batteries of equal voltage. The batteries are connected in series, so the overall voltage of the light is equal to the sum of the voltages of each battery. If the resistance of the light bulb's filament is 3.5 Ω and the current in the filament is 1.3 A, what is the total voltage across the filament? What is the voltage across each battery?

_____

PROBLEM

An electric car is equipped with a motor that can deliver 50 hp. The voltage across the motor's terminals equals 5.0×10^2 V, and the resistance in the motor's circuit is 7.5 Ω. How large is the current in the motor?

SOLUTION

Step 1: **List the given and unknown values.**

Given: *voltage, $V = 5.0 \times 10^2$ V*

resistance, $R = 7.5$ Ω

Unknown: *current, $I = ?$ A*

Step 2: **Write the equation for resistance, and rearrange it to solve for current.**

$$R = \frac{V}{I} \qquad I = \frac{V}{R}$$

Step 3: **Insert the known values into the equation, and solve.**

$$I = \frac{5.0 \times 10^2 \text{ V}}{7.5 \ \Omega}$$

$$I = 67 \text{ A}$$

| Math Skills *continued*

PRACTICE

6. A quadraphonic car stereo operates on electricity provided by the car's 12-V battery. Each channel of the stereo, which feeds the electric signal to one of the stereo's four speakers, has a resistance of about 4.1 Ω. What is the current in the circuit of each stereo channel?

_____

7. When resistors are connected end to end in a circuit, they are said to be in a series. The total resistance equals the sum of all the resistances. Suppose a string of lights has 25 bulbs. Each bulb has a resistance of 8.0 Ω. If the string is plugged into a 120-V outlet, how much current is in the entire set of lights?

_____

8. A chandelier has 10 sockets, each of which holds a 60.0-W light bulb. Each light bulb has a resistance of 240 Ω. However, the chandelier is wired so that the overall resistance provided by the 10-bulb circuit is only about 24.0 Ω. If the voltage across the chandelier's circuit is 115 V, how much current is in the chandelier?

_____

9. A window-unit air conditioner has an overall resistance of 22 Ω. If the voltage across the air conditioner equals 115 V, what is the current in the air conditioner's circuit?

_____

PROBLEM

A television set is plugged into a 120-V outlet. The current in the television is equal to 0.75 A. What is the overall resistance of the television set?

SOLUTION

Step 1: **List the given and unknown values.**

> **Given:** *voltage, V = 120 V*
>
> *current, I = 0.75 A*
>
> **Unknown:** *resistance, R = ?* Ω

Step 2: **Write the equation for resistance.**

$$R = \frac{V}{I}$$

| Math Skills *continued*

Step 3: Insert the known values into the equation, and solve.

$$R = \frac{V}{I} = \frac{120 \text{ V}}{0.75 \text{ A}}$$

$$R = 160 \text{ }|$$

PRACTICE

10. A medium-sized household oscillating fan draws 0.520 A of current when the potential difference across its motor is 120.0 V. How large is the fan's resistance?

_____

11. A refrigerator's circuit has a current equal to 0.647 A in it when the voltage across the circuit equals 116 V. What is the resistance of the circuit?

_____

MIXED PRACTICE

12. A portable, high-intensity lamp contains three bulbs with different power ratings: 150 W, 300 W, and 500 W. The resistance of each of these light bulbs decreases as the bulb's power output increases so that the 150-W bulb has a resistance of 96.0 $|$, the 300-W bulb has a resistance of 48.0 $|$, and the 500-W bulb has a resistance of 29.0 $|$. If the voltage across each bulb is 120.0 V, what is the current in each bulb?

_____

13. You have probably heard that high voltages are more dangerous than low voltages. To understand this, assume that your body has a resistance of 1.0×10^5 $|$. What voltages would have to be across your body to produce a current of 5.0 mA (milliamps, or 0.001 A), which would cause a tingling feeling; 10.0 mA, which would be a fatal amount of current; and 1.0 A?

_____

14. While in another country, you should always find out the voltage that is used in that country before you plug in an appliance. To understand the reason for this precaution, calculate the resistance of a laptop computer that is designed to draw 3.0 A at 115 V. Then, calculate the current that the same computer would draw if you plugged it into a 220-V outlet, which is common in countries other than the United States.

_____

Skills Worksheet

Math Skills

Electric Power

After you study each sample problem and solution, work out the practice problems on a separate sheet of paper. Write your answers in the spaces provided.

PROBLEM

An alarm clock uses 5.0 W of electric power. If the clock is plugged into a 120-V outlet, what electric current is in the clock's circuit?

SOLUTION

Step 1: List the given and unknown values.

Given: *voltage, V* = 120 V

power, P = 5.0 W

Unknown: *current, I* = ? A

Step 2: Write the equation for electric power, and rearrange it to solve for current.

$$P = VI \qquad I = \frac{P}{V}$$

Step 3: Insert the known values into the equation, and solve.

$$I = \frac{5.0 \text{ W}}{120 \text{ V}}$$

$$I = 4.2 \times 10^{-2} \text{ A}$$

PRACTICE

1. The headlights of an automobile have two power ratings: 45 W for the low beam and 65 W for the high beam. How much is the current in the headlight filament of a headlight bulb for both of these settings when 12 V is provided by the car battery?

_____

2. The heating coils of an electric stove are made of a high-resistance material so that the electricity that passes through the coils causes them to become red hot within a minute. The smaller coil draws 1,250 W of power, while the larger coil draws 2,100 W. The voltage provided across each coil is 240 V. What is the current in each coil?

_____

3. An electric mixer draws 200.0 W of power. If the mixer is plugged into an outlet across a voltage of 115 V, what current is in the mixer's circuit?

4. A bus built in 1905 used electricity produced by a gasoline-powered generator. The generator provided 33.6 kW of power to the bus. If the voltage across the electric motor was 440 V, what was the current in the motor?

5. Alternating current is used today because its voltage can be easily changed by a device called a transformer. Transformers are used both to increase the voltage of electricity, so that it can travel long distances, and to decrease the voltage, so that the electricity can be used in your house with relative safety. If the voltage across two wires is raised to 2.5×10^5 V, what is its current if 1.0×10^5 of power is provided?

PROBLEM

A high-intensity portable lantern is powered by several batteries that are connected in series. The lantern's bulb uses 96 W of power, while the current in the lantern is 4.0 A. Assuming that there is no power loss in the circuit, what is the total voltage of the batteries?

SOLUTION

Step 1: List the given and unknown values.

> **Given:** *power, P = 96 W*
> *current, I = 4.0 A*
> **Unknown:** *voltage, V = ? V*

Step 2: Write the equation for power, and rearrange it to solve for voltage.

$$P = VI \qquad V = \frac{P}{I}$$

Step 3: Insert the known values into the equation, and solve.

$$V = \frac{96 \text{ W}}{4.0 \text{ A}}$$

$$V = 24 \text{ V}$$

Name_____ Class _____ Date _____

| Math Skills *continued*

PRACTICE

6. A nightlight uses 4.00 W of power when plugged into an outlet. Assume that the only resistance in the circuit is provided by the light bulb's filament. The current in the circuit is 3.40×10^{-2}A. What is the voltage across the filament?

7. A portable power source is available for travelers who need electricity for appliances. The power source provides 54 W of power to operate an air compressor for inflating tires. This compressor draws 4.5 A of current when connected to the power supply. What is the voltage across the compressor?

8. A certain high-speed train is powered by 64 electric motors—one motor for each axle of each car. The power output of each motor is 185 kW. The current provided to each motor from overhead power lines is 7.4 A. What is the voltage across each motor?

9. A particular laser developed in 1995 at the University of Rochester, in New York, produced a beam of light that lasted for about one-billionth of a second. The power output of this beam was 6.0×10^{13} W. Assume that all of the electrical power was converted into light and that 8.0×10^6 A of current was needed to produce this beam. How large was the voltage that produced the current?

10. Fuel cells are chemical cells that combine hydrogen and oxygen gas to produce electrical energy. In recent years, a fuel cell has been developed that can generate 1.06×10^4 of power. If the cell produces a current of 16.3 A, what is the voltage across the cell?

PROBLEM

A generator produces electricity with a voltage of 2.5×10^4 V and a current of 20.0 A. How much power does the generator produce?

SOLUTION

Step 1: List the given and unknown values.

  Given: *voltage, $V = 2.5 \times 10^4$ V*

    current, $I = 20.0$ A

  Unknown: *power, $P = ?$ W*

Step 2: Write the equation for power.

  $P = VI$

Original content Copyright © by Holt, Rinehart and Winston. Additions and changes to the original content are the responsibility of the instructor.

Step 3: Insert the known values into the equation, and solve.

$$P = (2.5 \times 10^4 \, V) \times (20.0 \, A)$$
$$P = 5.0 \times 10^5 \, W$$

PROBLEM

A computer with a resistance of 57.5 │ has a power input of 230.0 W. Calculate the voltage across and current in the computer, using the formulas relating power to resistance.

SOLUTION

Step 1: List the given and unknown values.

Given: *power, P* = 230.0 W

resistance, R = 57.5 │

Unknown: *voltage, V* = ? V

current, I = ? A

Step 2: Write the equations for power in terms of resistance, and rearrange them to solve for voltage and current.

$$P = VI = V \times \frac{V}{R} = \frac{V^2}{R}$$
$$V = \sqrt{PR}$$
$$P = VI = (IR) \times I = I^2 R$$
$$I = \sqrt{\frac{P}{R}}$$

Step 3: Insert the known values into the equations, and solve.

$$V = \sqrt{(230.0 \, W) \times (57.5 \, \Omega)}$$
$$V = 115 \, V$$
$$I = \sqrt{\frac{230.0 \, W}{57.5 \, \Omega}}$$
$$I = 2.00 \, A$$

PRACTICE

11. A current of 5.83 A is used to produce the microwave radiation in a microwave oven. If the voltage across the oven is 120 V, how much power does the oven use?

_____

12. A vacuum cleaner's motor has a voltage of 120 V across its terminals and a current of 12 A. How much power does the vacuum cleaner use?

_____

13. A refrigerator uses a current of 0.62 A and a voltage of 116 V. How much power does the refrigerator use?

_____

14. An electric sports car was developed several years ago at Texas A & M University, in College Station, Texas. If the voltage required to operate the car was 720 V and the resistance was 0.30 V, how much power was needed for the car to run? (Hint: Express current in terms of voltage and resistance, and substitute this into the power equation.)

_____

MIXED PRACTICE

15. Electric power is often produced by a gas-powered generator. Suppose one of these generators has a power output of about 7.50×10^4 W. If the generator produces a voltage of 114 V, how much current is in the generator?

_____

16. Several appliances in a house contribute to the home's overall energy consumption. If a toaster ($R = 18.0$ |) an air conditioner ($R = 24.0$ |), and an electric lamp ($R = 192$ |) are all plugged into 120.0-V outlets, what is the power use of each appliance? What is the overall power use?

_____

17. There are 17 generators at Hoover Dam, each of which produces electricity with a voltage of 1.65×10^4 V and a current of 7.37×10^3 A. What is each generator's power output?

_____

18. One of the problems with transmitting electricity is that the resistance of the wire causes some energy to be transferred away as heat. This energy loss is equal to $I^2 R$. The loss can be reduced if the voltage can be increased so that the current decreases. Only alternating current can undergo this voltage increase, which is why AC is used for producing most electricity. Consider a power plant that produces 5.00×10^5 W of electricity. The wire has a resistance of 1.00×10^5 |. What is the power loss if the voltage is transmitted at 2.50×10^2 V? at 2.50×10^5 V?

_____

19. Power from mechanical work is often converted into electrical energy. Suppose you have a generator connected to a waterwheel that is turned by a waterfall. The waterfall is 25 m high, with 980 kg of water falling each second onto the waterwheel. If all of this mechanical energy is converted to electricity, how much power is generated? If the generated current is 20.0 A, what is the voltage?

_____